# VB.NET CODING

# ADVENTURES

*As simple as cut, paste and run –(well, almost).*
*Working with ManagementClass*

Richard Thomas Edwards

# CONTENTS

# What's Instore for you

## No storms on the horizon

This book is about using the System.Management.ManagementClass. It is also about the conservation of space and reusable code and how to get the most bang for your buck.

Let's face it, your time and your effort is worth money.

So is mine.

With that said, to book price within reason and make your code experience a positive one, the majority of the code needed to be organized in such a way that the bulk of redundancy code – like the code that initializes the management object collection – was used just once.

Just exactly how much

Therefore, that code - written just once - is placed in Appendix A. The GetManagementValue function will be placed in Appendix B. The stylesheets will be placed in Appendix C.

# Why do I keep using WMI?
## The method to my madness

UNLESS you are wanting to spend money, the last time I looked, free trumps paying for data resources you can use to power your outputs. Which is why I use it.

The other question I need to answer here is "ok, so when you create a database and a table with WMI, why do continually use 12 -or the memo field for every field entry?"

That is because I have no idea what the size of the values are going to be and based on my 20 years of experience, that datatype works just fine for every entry.

Now that you know the method to my madness, it is time to summarize what is about to be covered in the rest of this book:

*Access – create a database, table and populate it*

*ASP – both report and table mode, and horizontal and vertical orientations*

*ASPX – both report and table mode, and horizontal and vertical orientations*

*CSV - horizontal and vertical orientations*

*Element XML*

*Element XML for XSL*

*Excel Automation – both horizontal and vertical orientations*

*HTA – both report and table mode, and horizontal and vertical orientations*

*HTML – both report and table mode, and horizontal and vertical orientations*

*IDE DataGridView – both horizontal and vertical orientations*

*IDE Listview – both horizontal and vertical orientations*

*Schema XML*

*WPF DataGridView*

*WPF Listview*

*XSL - both report and table mode. In Multi-Line and Single line horizontal and Multi-Line and Single line vertical orientations*

Exactly how big would some of these routines be if they were not fragmented as I created them? Here's an example:

```
Dim cops As ConnectionOptions = New ConnectionOptions()
cops.Authentication = AuthenticationLevel.PacketPrivacy
cops.Impersonation = ImpersonationLevel.Impersonate
cops.Locale = "MS-0409"

Dim path As ManagementPath = New ManagementPath()
path.NamespacePath = "root\cimv2"
path.ClassName = "Win32_Process"
path.Server = "LocalHost"


Dim scope As ManagementScope = New ManagementScope(path, cops)
scope.Connect()

Dim mc As ManagementClass = New ManagementClass()
mc.Path = scope.Path
mc.Scope = scope

Dim moc As ManagementObjectCollection = mc.GetInstances()


Dim ws As Object = CreateObject("WScript.Shell")
Dim fso As Object = CreateObject("Scripting.FileSystemObject")
```

```
Dim    txtstream    As    Object    =    fso.OpenTextFile(ws.CurrentDirectory    +
"\Win32_Process.html", 2, true, -2)
    txtstream.WriteLine("<html xmlns='http://www.w3.org/1999/xhtml'>")
    txtstream.WriteLine("<head>")
    txtstream.WriteLine("<title>Win32_Process</title>")
    txtstream.WriteLine("<style type='text/css'>")
    txtstream.WriteLine("body")
    txtstream.WriteLine("{")
    txtstream.WriteLine("    PADDING-RIGHT: 0px;")
    txtstream.WriteLine("    PADDING-LEFT: 0px;")
    txtstream.WriteLine("    PADDING-BOTTOM: 0px;")
    txtstream.WriteLine("    MARGIN: 0px;")
    txtstream.WriteLine("    COLOR: #333;")
    txtstream.WriteLine("    PADDING-TOP: 0px;")
    txtstream.WriteLine("    FONT-FAMILY: verdana, arial, helvetica, sans-serif;")
    txtstream.WriteLine("}")
    txtstream.WriteLine("table")
    txtstream.WriteLine("{")
    txtstream.WriteLine("    BORDER-RIGHT: #999999 1px solid;")
    txtstream.WriteLine("    PADDING-RIGHT: 1px;")
    txtstream.WriteLine("    PADDING-LEFT: 1px;")
    txtstream.WriteLine("    PADDING-BOTTOM: 1px;")
    txtstream.WriteLine("    LINE-HEIGHT: 8px;")
    txtstream.WriteLine("    PADDING-TOP: 1px;")
    txtstream.WriteLine("    BORDER-BOTTOM: #999 1px solid;")
    txtstream.WriteLine("    BACKGROUND-COLOR: #eeeeee;")
    txtstream.WriteLine("
filter:progid:DXImageTransform.Microsoft.Shadow(color='silver',    Direction=135,
Strength=16")
    txtstream.WriteLine("}")
    txtstream.WriteLine("th")
    txtstream.WriteLine("{")
    txtstream.WriteLine("    BORDER-RIGHT: #999999 3px solid;")
```

```
txtstream.WriteLine("    PADDING-RIGHT: 6px;")
txtstream.WriteLine("    PADDING-LEFT: 6px;")
txtstream.WriteLine("    FONT-WEIGHT: Bold;")
txtstream.WriteLine("    FONT-SIZE: 14px;")
txtstream.WriteLine("    PADDING-BOTTOM: 6px;")
txtstream.WriteLine("    COLOR: darkred;")
txtstream.WriteLine("    LINE-HEIGHT: 14px;")
txtstream.WriteLine("    PADDING-TOP: 6px;")
txtstream.WriteLine("    BORDER-BOTTOM: #999 1px solid;")
txtstream.WriteLine("    BACKGROUND-COLOR: #eeeeee;")
txtstream.WriteLine("    FONT-FAMILY: font-family: Cambria, serif;")
txtstream.WriteLine("    FONT-SIZE: 12px;")
txtstream.WriteLine("    text-align: left;")
txtstream.WriteLine("    white-Space: nowrap;")
txtstream.WriteLine("}")
txtstream.WriteLine(".th")
txtstream.WriteLine("{")
txtstream.WriteLine("    BORDER-RIGHT: #999999 2px solid;")
txtstream.WriteLine("    PADDING-RIGHT: 6px;")
txtstream.WriteLine("    PADDING-LEFT: 6px;")
txtstream.WriteLine("    FONT-WEIGHT: Bold;")
txtstream.WriteLine("    PADDING-BOTTOM: 6px;")
txtstream.WriteLine("    COLOR: black;")
txtstream.WriteLine("    PADDING-TOP: 6px;")
txtstream.WriteLine("    BORDER-BOTTOM: #999 2px solid;")
txtstream.WriteLine("    BACKGROUND-COLOR: #eeeeee;")
txtstream.WriteLine("    FONT-FAMILY: font-family: Cambria, serif;")
txtstream.WriteLine("    FONT-SIZE: 10px;")
txtstream.WriteLine("    text-align: right;")
txtstream.WriteLine("    white-Space: nowrap;")
txtstream.WriteLine("}")
txtstream.WriteLine("td")
txtstream.WriteLine("{")
```

```
txtstream.WriteLine("    BORDER-RIGHT: #999999 3px solid;")
txtstream.WriteLine("    PADDING-RIGHT: 6px;")
txtstream.WriteLine("    PADDING-LEFT: 6px;")
txtstream.WriteLine("    FONT-WEIGHT: Normal;")
txtstream.WriteLine("    PADDING-BOTTOM: 6px;")
txtstream.WriteLine("    COLOR: navy;")
txtstream.WriteLine("    LINE-HEIGHT: 14px;")
txtstream.WriteLine("    PADDING-TOP: 6px;")
txtstream.WriteLine("    BORDER-BOTTOM: #999 1px solid;")
txtstream.WriteLine("    BACKGROUND-COLOR: #eeeeee;")
txtstream.WriteLine("    FONT-FAMILY: font-family: Cambria, serif;")
txtstream.WriteLine("    FONT-SIZE: 12px;")
txtstream.WriteLine("    text-align: left;")
txtstream.WriteLine("    white-Space: nowrap;")
txtstream.WriteLine("}")
txtstream.WriteLine("div")
txtstream.WriteLine("{")
txtstream.WriteLine("    BORDER-RIGHT: #999999 3px solid;")
txtstream.WriteLine("    PADDING-RIGHT: 6px;")
txtstream.WriteLine("    PADDING-LEFT: 6px;")
txtstream.WriteLine("    FONT-WEIGHT: Normal;")
txtstream.WriteLine("    PADDING-BOTTOM: 6px;")
txtstream.WriteLine("    COLOR: white;")
txtstream.WriteLine("    PADDING-TOP: 6px;")
txtstream.WriteLine("    BORDER-BOTTOM: #999 1px solid;")
txtstream.WriteLine("    BACKGROUND-COLOR: navy;")
txtstream.WriteLine("    FONT-FAMILY: font-family: Cambria, serif;")
txtstream.WriteLine("    FONT-SIZE: 10px;")
txtstream.WriteLine("    text-align: left;")
txtstream.WriteLine("    white-Space: nowrap;")
txtstream.WriteLine("}")
txtstream.WriteLine("span")
txtstream.WriteLine("{")
```

```
txtstream.WriteLine("   BORDER-RIGHT: #999999 3px solid;")
txtstream.WriteLine("   PADDING-RIGHT: 3px;")
txtstream.WriteLine("   PADDING-LEFT: 3px;")
txtstream.WriteLine("   FONT-WEIGHT: Normal;")
txtstream.WriteLine("   PADDING-BOTTOM: 3px;")
txtstream.WriteLine("   COLOR: white;")
txtstream.WriteLine("   PADDING-TOP: 3px;")
txtstream.WriteLine("   BORDER-BOTTOM: #999 1px solid;")
txtstream.WriteLine("   BACKGROUND-COLOR: navy;")
txtstream.WriteLine("   FONT-FAMILY: font-family: Cambria, serif;")
txtstream.WriteLine("   FONT-SIZE: 10px;")
txtstream.WriteLine("   text-align: left;")
txtstream.WriteLine("   white-Space: nowrap;")
txtstream.WriteLine("   display: inline-block;")
txtstream.WriteLine("   width: 100%;")
txtstream.WriteLine("}")
txtstream.WriteLine("textarea")
txtstream.WriteLine("{")
txtstream.WriteLine("   BORDER-RIGHT: #999999 3px solid;")
txtstream.WriteLine("   PADDING-RIGHT: 3px;")
txtstream.WriteLine("   PADDING-LEFT: 3px;")
txtstream.WriteLine("   FONT-WEIGHT: Normal;")
txtstream.WriteLine("   PADDING-BOTTOM: 3px;")
txtstream.WriteLine("   COLOR: white;")
txtstream.WriteLine("   PADDING-TOP: 3px;")
txtstream.WriteLine("   BORDER-BOTTOM: #999 1px solid;")
txtstream.WriteLine("   BACKGROUND-COLOR: navy;")
txtstream.WriteLine("   FONT-FAMILY: font-family: Cambria, serif;")
txtstream.WriteLine("   FONT-SIZE: 10px;")
txtstream.WriteLine("   text-align: left;")
txtstream.WriteLine("   white-Space: nowrap;")
txtstream.WriteLine("   width: 100%;")
txtstream.WriteLine("}")
```

```
txtstream.WriteLine("select")
txtstream.WriteLine("{")
txtstream.WriteLine("   BORDER-RIGHT: #999999 3px solid;")
txtstream.WriteLine("   PADDING-RIGHT: 6px;")
txtstream.WriteLine("   PADDING-LEFT: 6px;")
txtstream.WriteLine("   FONT-WEIGHT: Normal;")
txtstream.WriteLine("   PADDING-BOTTOM: 6px;")
txtstream.WriteLine("   COLOR: white;")
txtstream.WriteLine("   PADDING-TOP: 6px;")
txtstream.WriteLine("   BORDER-BOTTOM: #999 1px solid;")
txtstream.WriteLine("   BACKGROUND-COLOR: navy;")
txtstream.WriteLine("   FONT-FAMILY: font-family: Cambria, serif;")
txtstream.WriteLine("   FONT-SIZE: 10px;")
txtstream.WriteLine("   text-align: left;")
txtstream.WriteLine("   white-Space: nowrap;")
txtstream.WriteLine("   width: 100%;")
txtstream.WriteLine("}")
txtstream.WriteLine("input")
txtstream.WriteLine("{")
txtstream.WriteLine("   BORDER-RIGHT: #999999 3px solid;")
txtstream.WriteLine("   PADDING-RIGHT: 3px;")
txtstream.WriteLine("   PADDING-LEFT: 3px;")
txtstream.WriteLine("   FONT-WEIGHT: Bold;")
txtstream.WriteLine("   PADDING-BOTTOM: 3px;")
txtstream.WriteLine("   COLOR: white;")
txtstream.WriteLine("   PADDING-TOP: 3px;")
txtstream.WriteLine("   BORDER-BOTTOM: #999 1px solid;")
txtstream.WriteLine("   BACKGROUND-COLOR: navy;")
txtstream.WriteLine("   FONT-FAMILY: font-family: Cambria, serif;")
txtstream.WriteLine("   FONT-SIZE: 12px;")
txtstream.WriteLine("   text-align: left;")
txtstream.WriteLine("   display: table-cell;")
txtstream.WriteLine("   white-Space: nowrap;")
```

```vb
        txtstream.WriteLine("    width: 100%;")
        txtstream.WriteLine("}")
        txtstream.WriteLine("h1 {")
        txtstream.WriteLine("color: antiquewhite;")
        txtstream.WriteLine("text-shadow: 1px 1px black;")
        txtstream.WriteLine("padding: 3px;")
        txtstream.WriteLine("text-align: center;")
        txtstream.WriteLine("box-shadow: inset 2px 5px rgba(0,0,0,0.5), inset -2px -
2px 5px rgba(255,255,255,0.5);")
        txtstream.WriteLine("}")
        txtstream.WriteLine("</style>")
        txtstream.WriteLine("</head>")
        txtstream.WriteLine("<body>")
txtstream.WriteLine("<table border='0' Cellspacing='3' cellpadding = '3'>")
        Dim mocEnum As ManagementObjectCollection.ManagementObjectEnumerator
= moc.GetEnumerator()
        While (mocEnum.MoveNext())
            txtstream.WriteLine(" <tr> ")
            Dim mo As ManagementObject = mocEnum.Current()
            Dim proc As PropertyDataCollection = mo.Properties
            Dim    procEnum    As    PropertyDataCollection.PropertyDataEnumerator    =
proc.GetEnumerator()
            While (procEnum.MoveNext())
                Dim prop As PropertyData = procEnum.Current()
              txtstream.WriteLine(" <th align='left' nowrap>" + prop.Name + "</th> ")
            End While
            txtstream.WriteLine(" </tr> ")
            Exit While
        End While
        mocEnum.Reset()
        While (mocEnum.MoveNext())
            txtstream.WriteLine(" <tr> ")
            Dim mo As ManagementObject = mocEnum.Current()
```

```
        Dim proc As PropertyDataCollection = mo.Properties
        Dim   procEnum   As   PropertyDataCollection.PropertyDataEnumerator   =
proc.GetEnumerator()
        While (procEnum.MoveNext())
          Dim prop As PropertyData = procEnum.Current()
          Dim Value As String = GetManagementValue(prop.Name, mo)
            txtstream.WriteLine("  <td  style='font-family:Calibri,  Sans-Serif;font-
size:      12px;color:navy;'      align='left'      nowrap='nowrap'>"      +
GetManagementValue(prop.Name, mo) + "</td> ")
        End While
        txtstream.WriteLine(" </tr> ")
    End While
    txtstream.WriteLine("</table>")
    txtstream.WriteLine("</body>")
    txtstream.WriteLine("</html>")
    txtstream.close()


Function   GetManagementValue(ByVal   Name   As   String,   ByVal   mo   As
ManagementObject)

        Dim tempstr, pos, pName
        pName = vbTab & Name & " = "
        tempstr = mo.GetText(TextFormat.Mof)
        pos = InStr(tempstr, Name)
        If pos > 0 Then

          pos = pos + Len(Name) + 2
          tempstr = Mid(tempstr, pos, Len(tempstr))
          pos = InStr(tempstr, ";")
          tempstr = Mid(tempstr, 1, pos - 1)
          tempstr = Replace(tempstr, Chr(34), "")
          tempstr = Replace(tempstr, "{", "")
          tempstr = Replace(tempstr, "}", "")
```

```
tempstr = Trim(tempstr)

If Len(tempstr) > 13 Then

    If mo.Properties.Item(Name).Type = CimType.DateTime Then

        tempstr = Mid(tempstr, 5, 2) + "/" + _
            Mid(tempstr, 7, 2) + "/" + _
            Mid(tempstr, 1, 4) + " " + _
            Mid(tempstr, 9, 2) + ":" + _
            Mid(tempstr, 11, 2) + ":" + _
            Mid(tempstr, 13, 2)

    End If

End If

GetManagementValue = tempstr

Else

GetManagementValue = ""

End If

End Function
```

Since I'm reducing the enumerators back down to three simple routines

```
For each mo in moc
    For each prop in mo.Properties
    Next
```

```
        Exit For
    Next


And:


For each mo in moc
    For each prop in mo.Properties
    Next
Next


And:


For each mo in moc
    For each prop in mo.Properties
        For each mo1 in moc


        Next
    Next
    Exit For
Next
```

I am saving around 5 lines per enumeration and eliminating the GetManagementValue, a shorter Stylesheet, and the ManagementClass Code, you get this:


```
Dim ws As Object = CreateObject("WScript.Shell")
Dim fso As Object = CreateObject("Scripting.FileSystemObject")
Dim  txtstream  As  Object  =  fso.OpenTextFile(ws.CurrentDirectory  +
"\Win32_Process.html", 2, true, -2)
    txtstream.WriteLine("<html xmlns='http://www.w3.org/1999/xhtml'>")
    txtstream.WriteLine("<head>")
    txtstream.WriteLine("<title>Win32_Process</title>")
    txtstream.WriteLine("<style type='text/css'>")
    txtstream.WriteLine("th")
    txtstream.WriteLine("{")
    txtstream.WriteLine("    COLOR: darkred;")
```

```vb
        txtstream.WriteLine("    BACKGROUND-COLOR: white;")
        txtstream.WriteLine("    FONT-FAMILY:font-family: Cambria, serif;")
        txtstream.WriteLine("    FONT-SIZE: 12px;")
        txtstream.WriteLine("    text-align: left;")
        txtstream.WriteLine("    white-Space: nowrap;")
        txtstream.WriteLine("}")
        txtstream.WriteLine("td")
        txtstream.WriteLine("{")
        txtstream.WriteLine("    COLOR: navy;")
        txtstream.WriteLine("    BACKGROUND-COLOR: white;")
        txtstream.WriteLine("    FONT-FAMILY: font-family: Cambria, serif;")
        txtstream.WriteLine("    FONT-SIZE: 12px;")
        txtstream.WriteLine("    text-align: left;")
        txtstream.WriteLine("    white-Space: nowrap;")
        txtstream.WriteLine("}")
        txtstream.WriteLine("</style>")
        txtstream.WriteLine("</head>")
        txtstream.WriteLine("<body>")
txtstream.WriteLine("<table border='0' Cellspacing='3' cellpadding = '3'>")
        For each mo in moc
            txtstream.WriteLine(" <tr> ")
            For each prop in mo.Properties
                txtstream.WriteLine(" <th align='left' nowrap>" + prop.Name + "</th> ")
            Next
            txtstream.WriteLine(" </tr> ")
            Exit For
        Next
        For each mo in moc
            txtstream.WriteLine(" <tr> ")
            For each prop in mo.Properties
                Dim Value As String = GetManagementValue(prop.Name, mo)
```

```
        txtstream.WriteLine(" <td  style='font-family:Calibri,  Sans-Serif;font-
size:       12px;color:navy;'       align='left'       nowrap='nowrap'>"       +
GetManagementValue(prop.Name, mo) + "</td> ")
    Next
    txtstream.WriteLine(" </tr> ")
  Next
  txtstream.WriteLine("</table>")
  txtstream.WriteLine("</body>")
  txtstream.WriteLine("</html>")
  txtstream.close()
```

The full fledge example is 813 words . The example above: 154. The point: You
have a book that technically could be 500 pages in length if every example was
showing  the code needed for each to work.

# Access

```
Dim oAccess As Object = CreateObject("Access.Application")
oAccess.Visible = True
oAccess.NewCurrentDataBase(Application.StartupPath + "\Process.accdb", 0)
Dim db as Object = oAccess.CurrentDb
Dim tbldef As Object = db.CreateTableDef("Properties")
For each mo as ManagementObject in moc
    For each prop As PropertyData in mo.Properties
        Dim fld As Object = tbldef.CreateField(prop.Name, 12)
        fld.AllowZeroLength = True
        tbldef.Fields.Append(fld)
    Next
    Exit For
Next

db.TableDefs.Append(tbldef)

Dim rs As Object = db.OpenRecordset("Properties")
For Each mo As ManagementObject in moc
```

```
    rs.AddNew()
    For Each prop As PropertyData in mo.Properties
        rs.Fields(prop.Name).Value = GetManagementValue(prop.Name, mo)
    Next
    rs.Update()
Next
```

Horizontal Report

```
Dim ws As Object = CreateObject("WScript.Shell")
Dim fso As Object = CreateObject("Scripting.FileSystemObject")
Dim   txtstream   As   Object   =   fso.OpenTextFile(ws.CurrentDirectory   +
"\Win32_Process.asp", 2, true, -2)
txtstream.WriteLine("<html xmlns='http://www.w3.org/1999/xhtml'>")
txtstream.WriteLine("<head>")
txtstream.WriteLine("<title>Win32_Process</title>")
txtstream.WriteLine("<style type='text/css'>")
txtstream.WriteLine("th")
txtstream.WriteLine("{")
txtstream.WriteLine("   COLOR: darkred;")
txtstream.WriteLine("   BACKGROUND-COLOR: white;")
txtstream.WriteLine("   FONT-FAMILY:font-family: Cambria, serif;")
txtstream.WriteLine("   FONT-SIZE: 12px;")
txtstream.WriteLine("   text-align: left;")
txtstream.WriteLine("   white-Space: nowrap;")
txtstream.WriteLine("}")
txtstream.WriteLine("td")
txtstream.WriteLine("{")
txtstream.WriteLine("   COLOR: navy;")
txtstream.WriteLine("   BACKGROUND-COLOR: white;")
txtstream.WriteLine("   FONT-FAMILY: font-family: Cambria, serif;")
txtstream.WriteLine("   FONT-SIZE: 12px;")
txtstream.WriteLine("   text-align: left;")
txtstream.WriteLine("   white-Space: nowrap;")
```

```
txtstream.WriteLine("}")
txtstream.WriteLine("</style>")
txtstream.WriteLine("</head>")
txtstream.WriteLine("<body>")
txtstream.WriteLine("<table border='0' Cellspacing='3' cellpadding = '3'>")
txtstream.WriteLine("<%")
For each mo as ManagementObject in moc
    txtstream.WriteLine("Response.Write(""<tr>"" + vbcrlf)")
    For Each prop As PropertyData in mo.Properties
        txtstream.WriteLine("Response.Write(""<th   align='left'   nowrap>"" +
prop.Name + "</th>"" + vbcrlf)")
    Next
    txtstream.WriteLine("Response.Write(""</tr>"" + vbcrlf)")
    Exit For
Next
For Each mo As ManagementObject in moc
    txtstream.WriteLine("Response.Write(""<tr>"" + vbcrlf)")
    for each prop As PropertyData in mo.Properties
        txtstream.WriteLine("Response.Write(""<td   style='font-family:Calibri,
Sans-Serif;font-size:   12px;color:navy;'   align='left'   nowrap='nowrap'>"   +
GetManagementValue(prop.Name, mo) + "</td>"" + vbcrlf)")
    Next
    txtstream.WriteLine("Response.Write(""</tr>"" + vbcrlf)")
Next
txtstream.WriteLine("%>")
txtstream.WriteLine("</table>")
txtstream.WriteLine("</body>")
txtstream.WriteLine("</html>")
txtstream.close()
```

Vertical Report

```
Dim ws As Object = CreateObject("WScript.Shell")
Dim fso As Object = CreateObject("Scripting.FileSystemObject")
Dim txtstream As Object = fso.OpenTextFile(ws.CurrentDirectory +
"\Win32_Process.asp", 2, true, -2)
txtstream.WriteLine("<html xmlns='http://www.w3.org/1999/xhtml'>")
txtstream.WriteLine("<head>")
txtstream.WriteLine("<title>Win32_Process</title>")
txtstream.WriteLine("<style type='text/css'>")
txtstream.WriteLine("th")
txtstream.WriteLine("{")
txtstream.WriteLine("    COLOR: darkred;")
txtstream.WriteLine("    BACKGROUND-COLOR: white;")
txtstream.WriteLine("    FONT-FAMILY:font-family: Cambria, serif;")
txtstream.WriteLine("    FONT-SIZE: 12px;")
txtstream.WriteLine("    text-align: left;")
txtstream.WriteLine("    white-Space: nowrap;")
txtstream.WriteLine("}")
txtstream.WriteLine("td")
txtstream.WriteLine("{")
txtstream.WriteLine("    COLOR: navy;")
txtstream.WriteLine("    BACKGROUND-COLOR: white;")
txtstream.WriteLine("    FONT-FAMILY: font-family: Cambria, serif;")
txtstream.WriteLine("    FONT-SIZE: 12px;")
txtstream.WriteLine("    text-align: left;")
txtstream.WriteLine("    white-Space: nowrap;")
txtstream.WriteLine("}")
txtstream.WriteLine("</style>")
txtstream.WriteLine("</head>")
txtstream.WriteLine("<body>")
txtstream.WriteLine("<table border='0' Cellspacing='3' cellpadding = '3'>")
txtstream.WriteLine("<%")
For each mo as ManagementObject in moc
    For Each prop As PropertyData in mo.Properties
```

```
                txtstream.WriteLine("Response.Write(""<tr><th  align='left'  nowrap>"
+ prop.Name + "</th>""" + vbcrlf)")
            For Each mo1 As ManagementObject in moc
                txtstream.WriteLine("Response.Write(""<td                style='font-
family:Calibri,      Sans-Serif;font-size:      12px;color:navy;'      align='left'
nowrap='nowrap'>"   +   GetManagementValue(prop.Name,   mo1)   +   "</td>"""   +
vbcrlf)")
                Next
                txtstream.WriteLine("Response.Write(""</tr>""" + vbcrlf)")
        Next
        Exit For
    Next
    txtstream.WriteLine("%>")
    txtstream.WriteLine("</table>")
    txtstream.WriteLine("</body>")
    txtstream.WriteLine("</html>")
    txtstream.close()
```

## Horizontal Table

```
    Dim ws As Object = CreateObject("WScript.Shell")
    Dim fso As Object = CreateObject("Scripting.FileSystemObject")
    Dim   txtstream   As   Object   =   fso.OpenTextFile(ws.CurrentDirectory   +
"\Win32_Process.asp", 2, true, -2)
        txtstream.WriteLine("<html xmlns='http://www.w3.org/1999/xhtml'>")
        txtstream.WriteLine("<head>")
        txtstream.WriteLine("<title>Win32_Process</title>")
        txtstream.WriteLine("<style type='text/css'>")
        txtstream.WriteLine("th")
        txtstream.WriteLine("{")
        txtstream.WriteLine("   COLOR: darkred;")
        txtstream.WriteLine("   BACKGROUND-COLOR: white;")
        txtstream.WriteLine("   FONT-FAMILY:font-family: Cambria, serif;")
```

```
txtstream.WriteLine("    FONT-SIZE: 12px;")
txtstream.WriteLine("    text-align: left;")
txtstream.WriteLine("    white-Space: nowrap;")
txtstream.WriteLine("}")
txtstream.WriteLine("td")
txtstream.WriteLine("{")
txtstream.WriteLine("    COLOR: navy;")
txtstream.WriteLine("    BACKGROUND-COLOR: white;")
txtstream.WriteLine("    FONT-FAMILY: font-family: Cambria, serif;")
txtstream.WriteLine("    FONT-SIZE: 12px;")
txtstream.WriteLine("    text-align: left;")
txtstream.WriteLine("    white-Space: nowrap;")
txtstream.WriteLine("}")
txtstream.WriteLine("</style>")
txtstream.WriteLine("</head>")
txtstream.WriteLine("<body>")
txtstream.WriteLine("<table border='1' Cellspacing='3' cellpadding = '3'>")
txtstream.WriteLine("<%")
For each mo as ManagementObject in moc
    txtstream.WriteLine("Response.Write(""<tr>"" + vbcrlf)")
    For Each prop As PropertyData in mo.Properties
        txtstream.WriteLine("Response.Write(""<th  align='left'  nowrap>" +
prop.Name + "</th>"" + vbcrlf)")
    Next
    txtstream.WriteLine("Response.Write(""</tr>"" + vbcrlf)")
    Exit For
Next
For Each mo As ManagementObject in moc
    txtstream.WriteLine("Response.Write(""<tr>"" + vbcrlf)")
    for each prop As PropertyData in mo.Properties
        txtstream.WriteLine("Response.Write(""<td  style='font-family:Calibri,
Sans-Serif;font-size:  12px;color:navy;'  align='left'  nowrap='nowrap'>" +
GetManagementValue(prop.Name, mo) + "</td>"" + vbcrlf)")
```

```
        Next
        txtstream.WriteLine("Response.Write(""</tr>"" + vbcrlf)")
    Next
    txtstream.WriteLine("%>")
    txtstream.WriteLine("</table>")
    txtstream.WriteLine("</body>")
    txtstream.WriteLine("</html>")
    txtstream.close()
```

## Vertical Table

```
    Dim ws As Object = CreateObject("WScript.Shell")
    Dim fso As Object = CreateObject("Scripting.FileSystemObject")
    Dim txtstream As Object = fso.OpenTextFile(ws.CurrentDirectory +
"\Win32_Process.asp", 2, true, -2)
    txtstream.WriteLine("<html xmlns='http://www.w3.org/1999/xhtml'>")
    txtstream.WriteLine("<head>")
    txtstream.WriteLine("<title>Win32_Process</title>")
    txtstream.WriteLine("<style type='text/css'>")
    txtstream.WriteLine("th")
    txtstream.WriteLine("{")
    txtstream.WriteLine("   COLOR: darkred;")
    txtstream.WriteLine("   BACKGROUND-COLOR: white;")
    txtstream.WriteLine("   FONT-FAMILY:font-family: Cambria, serif;")
    txtstream.WriteLine("   FONT-SIZE: 12px;")
    txtstream.WriteLine("   text-align: left;")
    txtstream.WriteLine("   white-Space: nowrap;")
    txtstream.WriteLine("}")
    txtstream.WriteLine("td")
    txtstream.WriteLine("{")
    txtstream.WriteLine("   COLOR: navy;")
    txtstream.WriteLine("   BACKGROUND-COLOR: white;")
    txtstream.WriteLine("   FONT-FAMILY: font-family: Cambria, serif;")
```

```vb
txtstream.WriteLine("    FONT-SIZE: 12px;")
txtstream.WriteLine("    text-align: left;")
txtstream.WriteLine("    white-Space: nowrap;")
txtstream.WriteLine("}")
txtstream.WriteLine("</style>")
txtstream.WriteLine("</head>")
txtstream.WriteLine("<body>")
txtstream.WriteLine("<table border='1' Cellspacing='3' cellpadding = '3'>")
txtstream.WriteLine("<%")
For each mo as ManagementObject in moc
    For Each prop As PropertyData in mo.Properties
        txtstream.WriteLine("Response.Write(""<tr><th align='left' nowrap>"
+ prop.Name + "</th>""" + vbcrlf)")
        For Each mo1 As ManagementObject in moc
            txtstream.WriteLine("Response.Write(""<td                style='font-
family:Calibri,       Sans-Serif;font-size:      12px;color:navy;'       align='left'
nowrap='nowrap'>" + GetManagementValue(prop.Name, mo1) + "</td>"""  +
vbcrlf)")
        Next
        txtstream.WriteLine("Response.Write(""</tr>""" + vbcrlf)")
    Next
    Exit For
Next
txtstream.WriteLine("%>")
txtstream.WriteLine("</table>")
txtstream.WriteLine("</body>")
txtstream.WriteLine("</html>")
txtstream.close()
```

ASPX

```
Dim ws As Object = CreateObject("WScript.Shell")
Dim fso As Object = CreateObject("Scripting.FileSystemObject")
Dim txtstream As Object = fso.OpenTextFile(ws.CurrentDirectory +
"\Win32_Process.aspx", 2, true, -2)
txtstream.WriteLine("<!DOCTYPE html PUBLIC ""-//W3C//DTD XHTML 1.0
Transitional//EN""              ""http://www.w3.org/TR/xhtml1/DTD/xhtml1-
transitional.dtd"">")
txtstream.WriteLine("<html xmlns='http://www.w3.org/1999/xhtml'>")
txtstream.WriteLine("<title>Win32_Process</title>")
txtstream.WriteLine("<style type='text/css'>")
txtstream.WriteLine("th")
txtstream.WriteLine("{")
txtstream.WriteLine("    COLOR: darkred;")
txtstream.WriteLine("    BACKGROUND-COLOR: white;")
txtstream.WriteLine("    FONT-FAMILY:font-family: Cambria, serif;")
txtstream.WriteLine("    FONT-SIZE: 12px;")
txtstream.WriteLine("    text-align: left;")
txtstream.WriteLine("    white-Space: nowrap;")
txtstream.WriteLine("}")
txtstream.WriteLine("td")
txtstream.WriteLine("{")
txtstream.WriteLine("    COLOR: navy;")
txtstream.WriteLine("    BACKGROUND-COLOR: white;")
txtstream.WriteLine("    FONT-FAMILY: font-family: Cambria, serif;")
txtstream.WriteLine("    FONT-SIZE: 12px;")
txtstream.WriteLine("    text-align: left;")
txtstream.WriteLine("    white-Space: nowrap;")
txtstream.WriteLine("}")
txtstream.WriteLine("</style>")
```

```
txtstream.WriteLine("</head>")
txtstream.WriteLine("<body>")
txtstream.WriteLine("<table border='0' Cellspacing='3' cellpadding = '3'>")
txtstream.WriteLine("<%")
For each mo as ManagementObject in moc
    txtstream.WriteLine("Response.Write(""<tr>""" + vbcrlf)")
    For Each prop As PropertyData in mo.Properties
        txtstream.WriteLine("Response.Write(""<th  align='left'  nowrap>" +
prop.Name + "</th>""" + vbcrlf)")
    Next
    txtstream.WriteLine("Response.Write(""</tr>""" + vbcrlf)")
    Exit For
Next
For Each mo As ManagementObject in moc
    txtstream.WriteLine("Response.Write(""<tr>""" + vbcrlf)")
    for each prop As PropertyData in mo.Properties
        txtstream.WriteLine("Response.Write(""<td  style='font-family:Calibri,
Sans-Serif;font-size:  12px;color:navy;'  align='left'  nowrap='nowrap'>" +
GetManagementValue(prop.Name, mo) + "</td>""" + vbcrlf)")
    Next
    txtstream.WriteLine("Response.Write(""</tr>""" + vbcrlf)")
Next
txtstream.WriteLine("%>")
txtstream.WriteLine("</table>")
txtstream.WriteLine("</body>")
txtstream.WriteLine("</html>")
txtstream.close()
```

## Vertical Report

```
Dim ws As Object = CreateObject("WScript.Shell")
Dim fso As Object = CreateObject("Scripting.FileSystemObject")
```

```
Dim  txtstream  As  Object  =  fso.OpenTextFile(ws.CurrentDirectory  +
"\Win32_Process.aspx", 2, true, -2)
        txtstream.WriteLine("<!DOCTYPE html PUBLIC ""-//W3C//DTD XHTML 1.0
Transitional//EN""                ""http://www.w3.org/TR/xhtml1/DTD/xhtml1-
transitional.dtd"">")
        txtstream.WriteLine("<html xmlns='http://www.w3.org/1999/xhtml'>")
        txtstream.WriteLine("<title>Win32_Process</title>")
        txtstream.WriteLine("<style type='text/css'>")
        txtstream.WriteLine("th")
        txtstream.WriteLine("{")
        txtstream.WriteLine("   COLOR: darkred;")
        txtstream.WriteLine("   BACKGROUND-COLOR: white;")
        txtstream.WriteLine("   FONT-FAMILY:font-family: Cambria, serif;")
        txtstream.WriteLine("   FONT-SIZE: 12px;")
        txtstream.WriteLine("   text-align: left;")
        txtstream.WriteLine("   white-Space: nowrap;")
        txtstream.WriteLine("}")
        txtstream.WriteLine("td")
        txtstream.WriteLine("{")
        txtstream.WriteLine("   COLOR: navy;")
        txtstream.WriteLine("   BACKGROUND-COLOR: white;")
        txtstream.WriteLine("   FONT-FAMILY: font-family: Cambria, serif;")
        txtstream.WriteLine("   FONT-SIZE: 12px;")
        txtstream.WriteLine("   text-align: left;")
        txtstream.WriteLine("   white-Space: nowrap;")
        txtstream.WriteLine("}")
        txtstream.WriteLine("</style>")
        txtstream.WriteLine("</head>")
        txtstream.WriteLine("<body>")
        txtstream.WriteLine("<table border='0' Cellspacing='3' cellpadding = '3'>")
        txtstream.WriteLine("<%")
        For each mo as ManagementObject in moc
            For Each prop As PropertyData in mo.Properties
```

```
        txtstream.WriteLine("Response.Write(""<tr><th align='left' nowrap>"
+ prop.Name + "</th>""" + vbcrlf)")
            For Each mo1 As ManagementObject in moc
                txtstream.WriteLine("Response.Write(""<td                 style='font-
family:Calibri,      Sans-Serif;font-size:      12px;color:navy;'      align='left'
nowrap='nowrap'>"  +  GetManagementValue(prop.Name,  mo1)  +  "</td>"""  +
vbcrlf)")
              Next
            txtstream.WriteLine("Response.Write(""</tr>""" + vbcrlf)")
        Next
        Exit For
      Next
      txtstream.WriteLine("%>")
      txtstream.WriteLine("</table>")
      txtstream.WriteLine("</body>")
      txtstream.WriteLine("</html>")
      txtstream.close()
```

## Horizontal Table

```
      Dim ws As Object = CreateObject("WScript.Shell")
      Dim fso As Object = CreateObject("Scripting.FileSystemObject")
      Dim  txtstream  As  Object  =  fso.OpenTextFile(ws.CurrentDirectory  +
"\Win32_Process.aspx", 2, true, -2)
      txtstream.WriteLine("<!DOCTYPE html PUBLIC ""-//W3C//DTD XHTML 1.0
Transitional//EN""                ""http://www.w3.org/TR/xhtml1/DTD/xhtml1-
transitional.dtd"">")
      txtstream.WriteLine("<html xmlns='http://www.w3.org/1999/xhtml'>")
      txtstream.WriteLine("<title>Win32_Process</title>")
      txtstream.WriteLine("<style type='text/css'>")
      txtstream.WriteLine("th")
      txtstream.WriteLine("{")
```

```
txtstream.WriteLine("    COLOR: darkred;")
txtstream.WriteLine("    BACKGROUND-COLOR: white;")
txtstream.WriteLine("    FONT-FAMILY:font-family: Cambria, serif;")
txtstream.WriteLine("    FONT-SIZE: 12px;")
txtstream.WriteLine("    text-align: left;")
txtstream.WriteLine("    white-Space: nowrap;")
txtstream.WriteLine("}")
txtstream.WriteLine("td")
txtstream.WriteLine("{")
txtstream.WriteLine("    COLOR: navy;")
txtstream.WriteLine("    BACKGROUND-COLOR: white;")
txtstream.WriteLine("    FONT-FAMILY: font-family: Cambria, serif;")
txtstream.WriteLine("    FONT-SIZE: 12px;")
txtstream.WriteLine("    text-align: left;")
txtstream.WriteLine("    white-Space: nowrap;")
txtstream.WriteLine("}")
txtstream.WriteLine("</style>")
txtstream.WriteLine("</head>")
txtstream.WriteLine("<body>")
txtstream.WriteLine("<table border='1' Cellspacing='3' cellpadding = '3'>")
txtstream.WriteLine("<%")
For each mo as ManagementObject in moc
    txtstream.WriteLine("Response.Write(""<tr>"" + vbcrlf)")
    For Each prop As PropertyData in mo.Properties
        txtstream.WriteLine("Response.Write(""<th  align='left'  nowrap>"  +
prop.Name + "</th>"" + vbcrlf)")
    Next
    txtstream.WriteLine("Response.Write(""</tr>"" + vbcrlf)")
    Exit For
Next
For Each mo As ManagementObject in moc
    txtstream.WriteLine("Response.Write(""<tr>"" + vbcrlf)")
    for each prop As PropertyData in mo.Properties
```

```
        txtstream.WriteLine("Response.Write(""<td   style='font-family:Calibri,
Sans-Serif;font-size:    12px;color:navy;'    align='left'    nowrap='nowrap'>" +
GetManagementValue(prop.Name, mo) + "</td>""" + vbcrlf)")
        Next
            txtstream.WriteLine("Response.Write(""</tr>""" + vbcrlf)")
        Next
        txtstream.WriteLine("%>")
        txtstream.WriteLine("</table>")
        txtstream.WriteLine("</body>")
        txtstream.WriteLine("</html>")
        txtstream.close()
```

## Vertical Table

```
        Dim ws As Object = CreateObject("WScript.Shell")
        Dim fso As Object = CreateObject("Scripting.FileSystemObject")
        Dim  txtstream  As  Object  =  fso.OpenTextFile(ws.CurrentDirectory  +
"\Win32_Process.aspx", 2, true, -2)
        txtstream.WriteLine("<!DOCTYPE html PUBLIC ""-//W3C//DTD XHTML 1.0
Transitional//EN""                    ""http://www.w3.org/TR/xhtml1/DTD/xhtml1-
transitional.dtd"">")
        txtstream.WriteLine("<html xmlns='http://www.w3.org/1999/xhtml'>")
        txtstream.WriteLine("<title>Win32_Process</title>")
        txtstream.WriteLine("<style type='text/css'>")
        txtstream.WriteLine("th")
        txtstream.WriteLine("{")
        txtstream.WriteLine("   COLOR: darkred;")
        txtstream.WriteLine("   BACKGROUND-COLOR: white;")
        txtstream.WriteLine("   FONT-FAMILY:font-family: Cambria, serif;")
        txtstream.WriteLine("   FONT-SIZE: 12px;")
        txtstream.WriteLine("   text-align: left;")
        txtstream.WriteLine("   white-Space: nowrap;")
```

```vb
txtstream.WriteLine("}")
txtstream.WriteLine("td")
txtstream.WriteLine("{")
txtstream.WriteLine("   COLOR: navy;")
txtstream.WriteLine("   BACKGROUND-COLOR: white;")
txtstream.WriteLine("   FONT-FAMILY: font-family: Cambria, serif;")
txtstream.WriteLine("   FONT-SIZE: 12px;")
txtstream.WriteLine("   text-align: left;")
txtstream.WriteLine("   white-Space: nowrap;")
txtstream.WriteLine("}")
txtstream.WriteLine("</style>")
txtstream.WriteLine("</head>")
txtstream.WriteLine("<body>")
txtstream.WriteLine("<table border='1' Cellspacing='3' cellpadding = '3'>")
txtstream.WriteLine("<%")
For each mo as ManagementObject in moc
    For Each prop As PropertyData in mo.Properties
        txtstream.WriteLine("Response.Write(""<tr><th align='left' nowrap>"
+ prop.Name + "</th>""" + vbcrlf)")
        For Each mo1 As ManagementObject in moc
            txtstream.WriteLine("Response.Write(""<td            style='font-
family:Calibri,       Sans-Serif;font-size:      12px;color:navy;'      align='left'
nowrap='nowrap'>" + GetManagementValue(prop.Name,  mo1) + "</td>"""  +
vbcrlf)")
        Next
        txtstream.WriteLine("Response.Write(""</tr>""" + vbcrlf)")
    Next
    Exit For
Next
txtstream.WriteLine("%>")
txtstream.WriteLine("</table>")

txtstream.WriteLine("</body>")
```

```
txtstream.WriteLine("</html>")
txtstream.close()
```

# Element XML

```
Dim ws As Object = CreateObject("WScript.Shell")
Dim fso As Object = CreateObject("Scripting.FileSystemObject")
Dim txtstream As Object = fso.OpenTextFile(ws.CurrentDirectory +
"\Win32_Process.xml", 2, true, -2)

txtstream.WriteLine("<?xml version='1.0' encoding='iso-8859-1'?>")

txtstream.WriteLine("<data>")
```

```
For Each mo As ManagementObject in moc

    txtstream.WriteLine("<" + Tablename + ">")

    for each prop As PropertyData in mo.Properties

        txtstream.WriteLine("<" + prop.Name + ">" +
GetManagementValue(prop.Name, mo) + "</" + prop.Name + ">")

        next

        txtstream.WriteLine("</" + Tablename + ">")

next

txtstream.WriteLine("</data>")

txtstream.close
```

# Element XML For XSL

```
Dim ws As Object = CreateObject("WScript.Shell")

Dim fso As Object = CreateObject("Scripting.FileSystemObject")

Dim txtstream As Object = fso.OpenTextFile(ws.CurrentDirectory +
"\Win32_Process.xml", 2, true, -2)

txtstream.WriteLine("<?xml version='1.0' encoding='iso-8859-1'?>")
```

```
txtstream.WriteLine("<?xml-stylesheet type='Text/xsl'
href=""\Win32_Process.xsl""?>")

txtstream.WriteLine("<data>")

For Each mo As ManagementObject in moc

    txtstream.WriteLine("<process>")

    for each prop As PropertyData in mo.Properties

        txtstream.WriteLine("<" + prop.Name + ">" +
GetManagementValue(prop.Name, mo)+ "</" + prop.Name + ">")

        next

        txtstream.WriteLine("</process>")

next

txtstream.WriteLine("</data>")

txtstream.close
```

# Excel Automation

## Horizontal

```
Dim x As Integer = 1

Dim y As Integer = 2


Dim oExcel As Object = CreateObject("Excel.Application")
```

```
oExcel.Visible = True

Dim  wb As Object = oExcel.Workbooks.Add()

Dim  ws As Object = wb.Worksheets(0)

ws.Name = "Process"

y=2

x=1

For Each mo as ManagementObject in moc

    for each prop As PropertyData in mo.Properties

        ws.Cells.Item(1, x) = prop.Name

        x=x+1

    next

    Exit For

Next

x=1

For Each mo As ManagementObject in moc

    for each prop As PropertyData in mo.Properties)

        ws.Cells.Item(y, x) = GetManagementValue(prop.Name, mo)

        x=x+1

    next

    x= 1

    y=y+1

next

ws.Columns.HorizontalAlignment = -4131

ws.Columns.AutoFit()
```

## Vertical View

```
Dim x As Integer = 1
Dim y As Integer = 2


Dim oExcel As Object = CreateObject("Excel.Application")
oExcel.Visible = True
Dim  wb As Object = oExcel.Workbooks.Add()
Dim  ws As Object = wb.Worksheets(0)
ws.Name = "Process"
y=2
x=1
For Each mo as ManagementObject in moc
    for each prop As PropertyData in mo.Properties
      ws.Cells.Item(x, 1) = prop.Name
      x=x+1
    next
    Exit For
Next


x=1
For Each mo As ManagementObject in moc
    for each prop As PropertyData in mo.Properties)
      ws.Cells.Item(x, y) = GetManagementValue(prop.Name, mo)
      x=x+1
    next
```

```
    x= 1
    y=y+1
next
ws.Columns.HorizontalAlignment = -4131
ws.Columns.AutoFit()
```

# HTA

## Horizontal Report

```
Dim ws As Object = CreateObject("WScript.Shell")
Dim fso As Object = CreateObject("Scripting.FileSystemObject")
Dim txtstream As Object = fso.OpenTextFile(ws.CurrentDirectory +
"\Win32_Process.hta", 2, true, -2)
txtstream.WriteLine("<html xmlns='http://www.w3.org/1999/xhtml'>")
txtstream.WriteLine("<head>")
txtstream.WriteLine("<HTA:APPLICATION ")
txtstream.WriteLine("ID = ""Process"" ")
txtstream.WriteLine("APPLICATIONNAME = ""Process"" ")
txtstream.WriteLine("SCROLL = ""yes"" ")
txtstream.WriteLine("SINGLEINSTANCE = ""yes"" ")
txtstream.WriteLine("WINDOWSTATE = ""maximize"" >")
txtstream.WriteLine("<style type='text/css'>")
txtstream.WriteLine("th")
txtstream.WriteLine("{")
txtstream.WriteLine("    COLOR: darkred;")
txtstream.WriteLine("    BACKGROUND-COLOR: white;")
txtstream.WriteLine("    FONT-FAMILY:font-family: Cambria, serif;")
txtstream.WriteLine("    FONT-SIZE: 12px;")
txtstream.WriteLine("    text-align: left;")
txtstream.WriteLine("    white-Space: nowrap;")
txtstream.WriteLine("}")
txtstream.WriteLine("td")
txtstream.WriteLine("{")
txtstream.WriteLine("    COLOR: navy;")
```

```
txtstream.WriteLine("    BACKGROUND-COLOR: white;")
txtstream.WriteLine("    FONT-FAMILY: font-family: Cambria, serif;")
txtstream.WriteLine("    FONT-SIZE: 12px;")
txtstream.WriteLine("    text-align: left;")
txtstream.WriteLine("    white-Space: nowrap;")
txtstream.WriteLine("}")
txtstream.WriteLine("</style>")
txtstream.WriteLine("</head>")
txtstream.WriteLine("<body>")
txtstream.WriteLine("<table border='0' Cellspacing='3' cellpadding = '3'>")
For each mo as ManagementObject in moc
    txtstream.WriteLine("<tr>")
    For Each prop As PropertyData in mo.Properties
        txtstream.WriteLine("<th  align='left'  nowrap>" + prop.Name + "</th>")
    Next
    txtstream.WriteLine("</tr>")
    Exit For
Next
For Each mo As ManagementObject in moc
    txtstream.WriteLine("<tr>")
    for each prop As PropertyData in mo.Properties
        txtstream.WriteLine("<td  style='font-family:Calibri,  Sans-Serif;font-size:     12px;color:navy;'     align='left'     nowrap='nowrap'>" + GetManagementValue(prop.Name, mo) + "</td>")
    Next
    txtstream.WriteLine("</tr>")
Next
txtstream.WriteLine("</table>")
txtstream.WriteLine("</body>")
txtstream.WriteLine("</html>")
txtstream.close()
```

```
Dim ws As Object = CreateObject("WScript.Shell")
Dim fso As Object = CreateObject("Scripting.FileSystemObject")
Dim txtstream As Object = fso.OpenTextFile(ws.CurrentDirectory +
"\Win32_Process.hta", 2, true, -2)
txtstream.WriteLine("<html xmlns='http://www.w3.org/1999/xhtml'>")
txtstream.WriteLine("<head>")
txtstream.WriteLine("<HTA:APPLICATION ")
txtstream.WriteLine("ID = ""Process"" ")
txtstream.WriteLine("APPLICATIONNAME = ""Process"" ")
txtstream.WriteLine("SCROLL = ""yes"" ")
txtstream.WriteLine("SINGLEINSTANCE = ""yes"" ")
txtstream.WriteLine("WINDOWSTATE = ""maximize"" >")
txtstream.WriteLine("<style type='text/css'>")
txtstream.WriteLine("th")
txtstream.WriteLine("{")
txtstream.WriteLine("   COLOR: darkred;")
txtstream.WriteLine("   BACKGROUND-COLOR: white;")
txtstream.WriteLine("   FONT-FAMILY:font-family: Cambria, serif;")
txtstream.WriteLine("   FONT-SIZE: 12px;")
txtstream.WriteLine("   text-align: left;")
txtstream.WriteLine("   white-Space: nowrap;")
txtstream.WriteLine("}")
txtstream.WriteLine("td")
txtstream.WriteLine("{")
txtstream.WriteLine("   COLOR: navy;")
txtstream.WriteLine("   BACKGROUND-COLOR: white;")
txtstream.WriteLine("   FONT-FAMILY: font-family: Cambria, serif;")
txtstream.WriteLine("   FONT-SIZE: 12px;")
txtstream.WriteLine("   text-align: left;")
txtstream.WriteLine("   white-Space: nowrap;")
txtstream.WriteLine("}")
txtstream.WriteLine("</style>")
```

```
txtstream.WriteLine("</head>")
txtstream.WriteLine("<body>")
txtstream.WriteLine("<table border='0' Cellspacing='3' cellpadding = '3'>")
For each mo as ManagementObject in moc
    For Each prop As PropertyData in mo.Properties
        txtstream.WriteLine("<th align='left' nowrap>" + prop.Name +
"</th>")
        For Each mo1 As ManagementObject in moc
            txtstream.WriteLine("<td style='font-family:Calibri, Sans-Serif;font-
size:    12px;color:navy;'    align='left'    nowrap='nowrap'>"    +
GetManagementValue(prop.Name, mo1) + "</td>")
        Next
    Next
    txtstream.WriteLine("</tr>")
    Exit For
Next
txtstream.WriteLine("</table>")
txtstream.WriteLine("</body>")
txtstream.WriteLine("</html>")
txtstream.close()
```

## Horizontal Table

```
Dim ws As Object = CreateObject("WScript.Shell")
Dim fso As Object = CreateObject("Scripting.FileSystemObject")
Dim  txtstream  As  Object  =  fso.OpenTextFile(ws.CurrentDirectory  +
"\Win32_Process.hta", 2, true, -2)
txtstream.WriteLine("<html xmlns='http://www.w3.org/1999/xhtml'>")
txtstream.WriteLine("<head>")
txtstream.WriteLine("<HTA:APPLICATION ")
txtstream.WriteLine("ID = ""Process"" ")
txtstream.WriteLine("APPLICATIONNAME = ""Process"" ")
txtstream.WriteLine("SCROLL = ""yes"" ")
```

```
txtstream.WriteLine("SINGLEINSTANCE = ""yes"" ")
txtstream.WriteLine("WINDOWSTATE = ""maximize"" >")
txtstream.WriteLine("<style type='text/css'>")
txtstream.WriteLine("th")
txtstream.WriteLine("{")
txtstream.WriteLine("   COLOR: darkred;")
txtstream.WriteLine("   BACKGROUND-COLOR: white;")
txtstream.WriteLine("   FONT-FAMILY:font-family: Cambria, serif;")
txtstream.WriteLine("   FONT-SIZE: 12px;")
txtstream.WriteLine("   text-align: left;")
txtstream.WriteLine("   white-Space: nowrap;")
txtstream.WriteLine("}")
txtstream.WriteLine("td")
txtstream.WriteLine("{")
txtstream.WriteLine("   COLOR: navy;")
txtstream.WriteLine("   BACKGROUND-COLOR: white;")
txtstream.WriteLine("   FONT-FAMILY: font-family: Cambria, serif;")
txtstream.WriteLine("   FONT-SIZE: 12px;")
txtstream.WriteLine("   text-align: left;")
txtstream.WriteLine("   white-Space: nowrap;")
txtstream.WriteLine("}")
txtstream.WriteLine("</style>")
txtstream.WriteLine("</head>")
txtstream.WriteLine("<body>")
txtstream.WriteLine("<table border='1' Cellspacing='3' cellpadding = '3'>")
For each mo as ManagementObject in moc
   txtstream.WriteLine("<tr>")
   For Each prop As PropertyData in mo.Properties
      txtstream.WriteLine("<th   align='left'   nowrap>" +   prop.Name   +
"</th>")
   Next
   txtstream.WriteLine("</tr>")
   Exit For
```

```
        Next
        For Each mo As ManagementObject in moc
            txtstream.WriteLine("<tr>")
            for each prop As PropertyData in mo.Properties
                txtstream.WriteLine("<td   style='font-family:Calibri,   Sans-Serif;font-
size:       12px;color:navy;'        align='left'        nowrap='nowrap'>"        +
GetManagementValue(prop.Name, mo) + "</td>")
            Next
            txtstream.WriteLine("</tr>")
        Next
        txtstream.WriteLine("</table>")
        txtstream.WriteLine("</body>")
        txtstream.WriteLine("</html>")
        txtstream.close()
```

## Vertical Table

```
        Dim ws As Object = CreateObject("WScript.Shell")
        Dim fso As Object = CreateObject("Scripting.FileSystemObject")
        Dim   txtstream   As   Object   =   fso.OpenTextFile(ws.CurrentDirectory   +
"\Win32_Process.hta", 2, true, -2)
        txtstream.WriteLine("<html xmlns='http://www.w3.org/1999/xhtml'>")
        txtstream.WriteLine("<head>")
        txtstream.WriteLine("<HTA:APPLICATION ")
        txtstream.WriteLine("ID = ""Process"" ")
        txtstream.WriteLine("APPLICATIONNAME = ""Process"" ")
        txtstream.WriteLine("SCROLL = ""yes"" ")
        txtstream.WriteLine("SINGLEINSTANCE = ""yes"" ")
        txtstream.WriteLine("WINDOWSTATE = ""maximize"" >")
        txtstream.WriteLine("<style type='text/css'>")
        txtstream.WriteLine("th")
        txtstream.WriteLine("{")
        txtstream.WriteLine("   COLOR: darkred;")
```

```
txtstream.WriteLine("   BACKGROUND-COLOR: white;")
txtstream.WriteLine("   FONT-FAMILY:font-family: Cambria, serif;")
txtstream.WriteLine("   FONT-SIZE: 12px;")
txtstream.WriteLine("   text-align: left;")
txtstream.WriteLine("   white-Space: nowrap;")
txtstream.WriteLine("}")
txtstream.WriteLine("td")
txtstream.WriteLine("{")
txtstream.WriteLine("   COLOR: navy;")
txtstream.WriteLine("   BACKGROUND-COLOR: white;")
txtstream.WriteLine("   FONT-FAMILY: font-family: Cambria, serif;")
txtstream.WriteLine("   FONT-SIZE: 12px;")
txtstream.WriteLine("   text-align: left;")
txtstream.WriteLine("   white-Space: nowrap;")
txtstream.WriteLine("}")
txtstream.WriteLine("</style>")
txtstream.WriteLine("</head>")
txtstream.WriteLine("<body>")
txtstream.WriteLine("<table border='1' Cellspacing='3' cellpadding = '3'>")
For each mo as ManagementObject in moc
    For Each prop As PropertyData in mo.Properties
        txtstream.WriteLine("<th align='left' nowrap>" + prop.Name + "</th>")
        For Each mo1 As ManagementObject in moc
            txtstream.WriteLine("<td style='font-family:Calibri, Sans-Serif;font-size: 12px;color:navy;' align='left' nowrap='nowrap'>" + GetManagementValue(prop.Name, mo1) + "</td>")
        Next
    Next
    txtstream.WriteLine("</tr>")
    Exit For
Next
txtstream.WriteLine("</table>")
```

```
txtstream.WriteLine("</body>")
txtstream.WriteLine("</html>")
txtstream.close()
```

# HTML

```
Dim ws As Object = CreateObject("WScript.Shell")
Dim fso As Object = CreateObject("Scripting.FileSystemObject")
Dim txtstream As Object = fso.OpenTextFile(ws.CurrentDirectory +
"\Win32_Process.html", 2, true, -2)
    txtstream.WriteLine("<html xmlns='http://www.w3.org/1999/xhtml'>")
    txtstream.WriteLine("<head>")
    txtstream.WriteLine("<title>Win32_Process</title>")
    txtstream.WriteLine("<style type='text/css'>")
    txtstream.WriteLine("th")
    txtstream.WriteLine("{")
    txtstream.WriteLine("   COLOR: darkred;")
    txtstream.WriteLine("   BACKGROUND-COLOR: white;")
    txtstream.WriteLine("   FONT-FAMILY:font-family: Cambria, serif;")
    txtstream.WriteLine("   FONT-SIZE: 12px;")
    txtstream.WriteLine("   text-align: left;")
    txtstream.WriteLine("   white-Space: nowrap;")
    txtstream.WriteLine("}")
    txtstream.WriteLine("td")
    txtstream.WriteLine("{")
    txtstream.WriteLine("   COLOR: navy;")
    txtstream.WriteLine("   BACKGROUND-COLOR: white;")
    txtstream.WriteLine("   FONT-FAMILY: font-family: Cambria, serif;")
```

```
txtstream.WriteLine("    FONT-SIZE: 12px;")
txtstream.WriteLine("    text-align: left;")
txtstream.WriteLine("    white-Space: nowrap;")
txtstream.WriteLine("}")
txtstream.WriteLine("</style>")
txtstream.WriteLine("</head>")
txtstream.WriteLine("<body>")
txtstream.WriteLine("<table border='0' Cellspacing='3' cellpadding = '3'>")
For each mo as ManagementObject in moc
    txtstream.WriteLine("<tr>")
    For Each prop As PropertyData in mo.Properties
        txtstream.WriteLine("<th  align='left'  nowrap>" + prop.Name +
"</th>")
    Next
    txtstream.WriteLine("</tr>")
    Exit For
Next
For Each mo As ManagementObject in moc
    txtstream.WriteLine("<tr>")
    for each prop As PropertyData in mo.Properties
        txtstream.WriteLine("<td  style='font-family:Calibri,  Sans-Serif;font-
size:    12px;color:navy;'    align='left'    nowrap='nowrap'>"    +
GetManagementValue(prop.Name, mo) + "</td>")
    Next
    txtstream.WriteLine("</tr>")
Next
txtstream.WriteLine("</table>")
txtstream.WriteLine("</body>")
txtstream.WriteLine("</html>")
txtstream.close()
```

```
Dim ws As Object = CreateObject("WScript.Shell")
Dim fso As Object = CreateObject("Scripting.FileSystemObject")
Dim txtstream As Object = fso.OpenTextFile(ws.CurrentDirectory +
"\Win32_Process.html", 2, true, -2)
txtstream.WriteLine("<html xmlns='http://www.w3.org/1999/xhtml'>")
txtstream.WriteLine("<head>")
txtstream.WriteLine("<title>Win32_Process</title>")
txtstream.WriteLine("<style type='text/css'>")
txtstream.WriteLine("th")
txtstream.WriteLine("{")
txtstream.WriteLine("   COLOR: darkred;")
txtstream.WriteLine("   BACKGROUND-COLOR: white;")
txtstream.WriteLine("   FONT-FAMILY:font-family: Cambria, serif;")
txtstream.WriteLine("   FONT-SIZE: 12px;")
txtstream.WriteLine("   text-align: left;")
txtstream.WriteLine("   white-Space: nowrap;")
txtstream.WriteLine("}")
txtstream.WriteLine("td")
txtstream.WriteLine("{")
txtstream.WriteLine("   COLOR: navy;")
txtstream.WriteLine("   BACKGROUND-COLOR: white;")
txtstream.WriteLine("   FONT-FAMILY: font-family: Cambria, serif;")
txtstream.WriteLine("   FONT-SIZE: 12px;")
txtstream.WriteLine("   text-align: left;")
txtstream.WriteLine("   white-Space: nowrap;")
txtstream.WriteLine("}")
txtstream.WriteLine("</style>")
txtstream.WriteLine("</head>")
txtstream.WriteLine("<body>")
txtstream.WriteLine("<table border='0' Cellspacing='3' cellpadding = '3'>")
For each mo as ManagementObject in moc
```

```
        For Each prop As PropertyData in mo.Properties
            txtstream.WriteLine("<th   align='left'   nowrap>" +   prop.Name   +
"</th>”)
            For Each mo1 As ManagementObject in moc
                txtstream.WriteLine("<td style='font-family:Calibri, Sans-Serif;font-
size:      12px;color:navy;'       align='left'       nowrap='nowrap'>"       +
GetManagementValue(prop.Name, mo1) + "</td>")
            Next
        Next
        txtstream.WriteLine("</tr>")
        Exit For
    Next
    txtstream.WriteLine("</table>")
    txtstream.WriteLine("</body>")
    txtstream.WriteLine("</html>")
    txtstream.close()
```

## Horizontal Table

```
    Dim ws As Object = CreateObject("WScript.Shell")
    Dim fso As Object = CreateObject("Scripting.FileSystemObject")
    Dim  txtstream  As  Object  =  fso.OpenTextFile(ws.CurrentDirectory  +
"\Win32_Process.html", 2, true, -2)
    txtstream.WriteLine("<html xmlns='http://www.w3.org/1999/xhtml'>")
    txtstream.WriteLine("<head>")
    txtstream.WriteLine("<title>Win32_Process</title>")
    txtstream.WriteLine("<style type='text/css'>")
    txtstream.WriteLine("th")
    txtstream.WriteLine("{")
    txtstream.WriteLine("    COLOR: darkred;")
    txtstream.WriteLine("    BACKGROUND-COLOR: white;")
    txtstream.WriteLine("    FONT-FAMILY:font-family: Cambria, serif;")
```

```
txtstream.WriteLine("   FONT-SIZE: 12px;")
txtstream.WriteLine("   text-align: left;")
txtstream.WriteLine("   white-Space: nowrap;")
txtstream.WriteLine("}")
txtstream.WriteLine("td")
txtstream.WriteLine("{")
txtstream.WriteLine("   COLOR: navy;")
txtstream.WriteLine("   BACKGROUND-COLOR: white;")
txtstream.WriteLine("   FONT-FAMILY: font-family: Cambria, serif;")
txtstream.WriteLine("   FONT-SIZE: 12px;")
txtstream.WriteLine("   text-align: left;")
txtstream.WriteLine("   white-Space: nowrap;")
txtstream.WriteLine("}")
txtstream.WriteLine("</style>")
txtstream.WriteLine("</head>")
txtstream.WriteLine("<body>")
txtstream.WriteLine("<table border='1' Cellspacing='3' cellpadding = '3'>")
For each mo as ManagementObject in moc
    txtstream.WriteLine("<tr>")
    For Each prop As PropertyData in mo.Properties
        txtstream.WriteLine("<th   align='left'   nowrap>"   +   prop.Name   +
"</th>")
    Next
    txtstream.WriteLine("</tr>")
    Exit For
Next
For Each mo As ManagementObject in moc
    txtstream.WriteLine("<tr>")
    for each prop As PropertyData in mo.Properties
        txtstream.WriteLine("<td   style='font-family:Calibri,   Sans-Serif;font-
size:   12px;color:navy;'   align='left'   nowrap='nowrap'>"   +
GetManagementValue(prop.Name, mo) + "</td>")
    Next
```

```
        txtstream.WriteLine("</tr>")
    Next
    txtstream.WriteLine("</table>")
    txtstream.WriteLine("</body>")
    txtstream.WriteLine("</html>")
    txtstream.close()
```

## Vertical Table

```
    Dim ws As Object = CreateObject("WScript.Shell")
    Dim fso As Object = CreateObject("Scripting.FileSystemObject")
    Dim  txtstream  As  Object  =  fso.OpenTextFile(ws.CurrentDirectory  +
"\Win32_Process.html", 2, true, -2)
    txtstream.WriteLine("<html xmlns='http://www.w3.org/1999/xhtml'>")
    txtstream.WriteLine("<head>")
    txtstream.WriteLine("<title>Win32_Process</title>")
    txtstream.WriteLine("<style type='text/css'>")
    txtstream.WriteLine("th")
    txtstream.WriteLine("{")
    txtstream.WriteLine("   COLOR: darkred;")
    txtstream.WriteLine("   BACKGROUND-COLOR: white;")
    txtstream.WriteLine("   FONT-FAMILY:font-family: Cambria, serif;")
    txtstream.WriteLine("   FONT-SIZE: 12px;")
    txtstream.WriteLine("   text-align: left;")
    txtstream.WriteLine("   white-Space: nowrap;")
    txtstream.WriteLine("}")
    txtstream.WriteLine("td")
    txtstream.WriteLine("{")
    txtstream.WriteLine("   COLOR: navy;")
    txtstream.WriteLine("   BACKGROUND-COLOR: white;")
    txtstream.WriteLine("   FONT-FAMILY: font-family: Cambria, serif;")
    txtstream.WriteLine("   FONT-SIZE: 12px;")
```

```
txtstream.WriteLine("    text-align: left;")
txtstream.WriteLine("    white-Space: nowrap;")
txtstream.WriteLine("}")
txtstream.WriteLine("</style>")
txtstream.WriteLine("</head>")
txtstream.WriteLine("<body>")
txtstream.WriteLine("<table border='1' Cellspacing='3' cellpadding = '3'>")
For each mo as ManagementObject in moc
    For Each prop As PropertyData in mo.Properties
        txtstream.WriteLine("<th   align='left'   nowrap>" + prop.Name +
"</th>")
        For Each mo1 As ManagementObject in moc
            txtstream.WriteLine("<td style='font-family:Calibri, Sans-Serif;font-
size:      12px;color:navy;'      align='left'      nowrap='nowrap'>"      +
GetManagementValue(prop.Name, mo1) + "</td>")
        Next
    Next
    txtstream.WriteLine("</tr>")
    Exit For
Next
txtstream.WriteLine("</table>")
txtstream.WriteLine("</body>")
txtstream.WriteLine("</html>")
txtstream.close()
```

# IDE DataGridView

```
Dim x As Integer = 0
Dim y As Integer = 0
```

Horizontal View

```
For each prop As PropertyData in mo.Properties
    DataGridView1.Columns.Add(prop.Name, prop.Name)
Next
For Each mo As ManagementObject in moc
    DataGridView1.Rows.Add()
    For each prop As PropertyData in mo.Properties
        DataGridView1.Rows(y).Cells(x).Value = GetManagementValue(prop.Name,
mo)
        x = x + 1
    Next
    x = 0
    y = y + 1
Next
```

Vertical View

```
DataGridView1.Columns.Add("Property Name", "Property Name")
For Each mo As ManagementObject in moc
    DataGridView1.Columns.Add("Row(" & x & ")", "Row(" & x & ")")
    x = x + 1
Next

x = 1

For each prop As PropertyData in mo.Properties
    DataGridView1.Rows.Add()
    DataGridView1.Rows(y).Cells(0).Value = prop.Name
    For Each mo As ManagementObject in moc
        DataGridView1.Rows(y).Cells(x).Value = GetManagementValue(prop.Name,
mo)
        x = x + 1
    Next
    x = 1
    y = y + 1
Next
```

# IDE Listview

## Horizontal View

```
For each prop As PropertyData in mo.Properties
    ListView1.Columns.Add(prop.Name)
Next

Dim li As ListViewItem = Nothing
For Each mo As ManagementObject in moc
    For each prop As PropertyData in mo.Properties
        Dim value As String =
GetManagementValue(prop.Name, mo)
        If x = 0 Then
            li = ListView1.Items.Add(value)
        Else
            li.SubItems.Add(value)
        End If
        x = x + 1
    Next
    x = 0
Next
```

## Vertical View

```
x = 0
Dim li As ListViewItem = Nothing
ListView1.Columns.Add("Property Name", 200)
For Each mo As ManagementObject in moc
    ListView1.Columns.Add("Row(" & x & ")", 480)
    x = x + 1
Next

x = 1
```

```
For each prop As PropertyData in mo.Properties
    li = ListView1.Items.Add(prop.Name)
    For Each mo As ManagementObject in moc
        Dim value As String =
GetManagementValue(prop.Name, mo)
            li.SubItems.Add(value)
    Next
Next
```

# Schema XML

```
Dim ws As Object = CreateObject("WScript.Shell")

Dim fso As Object = CreateObject("Scripting.FileSystemObject")

Dim txtstream As Object = fso.OpenTextFile(ws.CurrentDirectory +
"\Win32_Process.xml", 2, true, -2)

txtstream.WriteLine("<?xml version='1.0' encoding='iso-8859-1'?>")

txtstream.WriteLine("<data>")

For Each mo As ManagementObject in moc

    txtstream.WriteLine("<" + Tablename + ">")

    for each prop As PropertyData in mo.Properties

        txtstream.WriteLine("<" + prop.Name + ">" +
GetManagementValue(prop.Name, mo)+ "</" + prop.Name + ">")

    next

        txtstream.WriteLine("</" + Tablename + ">")

next

txtstream.WriteLine("</data>")

txtstream.close


Dim rs1 As Object = CreateObject("ADODB.Recordset")

rs1.ActiveConnection = "Provider=MSDAOSP; Data Source=msxml2.DSOControl"

rs1.Open(ws.CurrentDirectory + "\Win32_Process.xml")


if(fso.FileExists(ws.CurrentDirectory + "\Win32_Process_Schema.xml") = true)
```

```
    fso.DeleteFile(ws.CurrentDirectory + "\Win32_Process_Schema.xml")
end if

rs.Save(ws.CurrentDirectory + "\Win32_Process_Schema.xml, 1)
```

# WPF DataGridView

The code below is using WbemScripting to connect to the local machine. In this example, we're using the Get Interface WbemScripting.SWbemServices must gather the information from WMI's Win32_Process. All standard stuff.

What is not so standard is the dynamic creation of a Dataset and Datatable. When done dynamically, an empty Datatable is added to the dataset as seen below.

Horizontal

```
Dim l As Object = CreateObject("WbemScripting.SWbemLocator")
Dim svc As Object = l.ConnectServer("LocalHost", "root\cimv2")
svc.Security_.AuthenticationLevel = 6
svc.Security_.ImpersonationLevel = 4

Dim objs As Object = svc.ExecQuery("Select * from Win32_Process")

Dim ds As New System.Data.DataSet
Dim dt As New System.Data.DataTable
ds.Tables.Add(dt)


For Each mo As ManagementObject in moc
    For each prop As PropertyData in mo.Properties
      ds.Tables(0).Columns.Add(prop.Name)
    Next
```

```
        Exit For
    Next

    For Each mo As ManagementObject in moc
        Dim dr As System.Data.DataRow = ds.Tables(0).NewRow
        For each prop As PropertyData in mo.Properties
            dr(prop.Name) = GetManagementValue(prop.Name, mo)
        Next
        ds.Tables(0).Rows.Add(dr)
    Next

    DataGrid1.ItemsSource = ds.Tables(0).DefaultView
```

Vertical

```
    Dim ds As New System.Data.DataSet
    Dim dt As New System.Data.DataTable
    ds.Tables.Add(dt)
    ds.Tables(0).Columns.Add("Property Name")

    Dim x As Integer = 0
    For each mo as ManagementObject in moc
        ds.Tables(0).Columns.Add("Row" & x)
        X = X + 1
    Loop

    X = 0
    For each mo as ManagementObject in moc
        For each prop as PropertyData in mo.Properties
            Dim dr As System.Data.DataRow = ds.Tables(0).NewRow
            dr(0) = prop.Name
            For each mo1 as ManagementObject in moc
                dr(x + 1) = GetManagementValue(prop.Name, mo1)
```

```
            x = x + 1
        Next
        x = 0
        ds.Tables(0).Rows.Add(dr)
    Next
    Exit For
Next

DataGrid1.ItemsSource = ds.Tables(0).DefaultView
```

# WPF Listview

Much like the WPF DataGridView, the WbemScripting can dynamically and information to the Listview. But this time, we're dynamically driving the

Horizontal

```
Dim gv As New GridView


    Dim ds As New System.Data.DataSet
    Dim dt As New System.Data.DataTable
    ds.Tables.Add(dt)

    For each mo as ManagementObject in moc
        For each prop as PropertyData in mo.Properties
            ds.Tables(0).Columns.Add(prop.Name)
            Dim b As New Binding(prop.Name)
            Dim c As New GridViewColumn
            c.Header = prop.Name
            c.DisplayMemberBinding = b
            gv.Columns.Add(c)
        Next
```

```vbnet
        Exit For
    Next

    For each mo as ManagementObject in moc
        Dim dr As System.Data.DataRow = ds.Tables(0).NewRow
        For each prop as PropertyData in mo.Properties
            dr(prop.Name) = GetManagementValue(prop.Name, mo)
        Next
        ds.Tables(0).Rows.Add(dr)
    Next
    Listview1.View = gv

    Listview1.ItemsSource = ds.Tables(0).DefaultView

Vertical

    Dim gv As New GridView

    Dim ds As New System.Data.DataSet
    Dim dt As New System.Data.DataTable
    ds.Tables.Add(dt)

    ds.Tables(0).Columns.Add("Property Name")

    Dim x As Integer = 0
    For each mo as ManagementObject in moc
        ds.Tables(0).Columns.Add("Row" & x)
        x = x + 1
    Next

    x = 0
```

```
For each mo as ManagementObject in moc
    Dim dr As System.Data.DataRow = ds.Tables(0).NewRow
    For each prop as PropertyData in mo.Properties
        Dim dr As System.Data.DataRow = ds.Tables(0).NewRow
        dr(0) = prop.Name
        For each mo1 as ManagementObject in moc
            dr(x + 1) = GetManagementValue(prop.Name, mo1)
            x = x + 1
        Next
        x = 0
        ds.Tables(0).Rows.Add(dr)
    Next
    Exit For
Next

DataGrid1.ItemsSource = ds.Tables(0).DefaultView
```

# XSL

## SINGLE LINE HORIZONTAL

```
Dim  ws As Object  = CreateObject("WScript.Shell")

Dim fso As Object = CreateObject("Scripting.FileSystemObject")

Dim txtstream As Object = fso.OpenTextFile(ws.CurrentDirectory + "\Process.xsl", 2,
true, -2)

txtstream.WriteLine("<?xml version=""1.0" " encoding=""UTF-8" "?>")

txtstream.WriteLine("<xsl:stylesheet version=""1.0""
xmlns:xsl=""http://www.w3.org/1999/XSL/Transform" ">")

txtstream.WriteLine("<xsl:template match=""/""">")

txtstream.WriteLine("<html>")

txtstream.WriteLine("<head>")

txtstream.WriteLine("<title>Products</title>")

txtstream.WriteLine("<style type='text/css'>")

txtstream.WriteLine("th")

txtstream.WriteLine("{")
```

```
txtstream.WriteLine("    COLOR: darkred;")
txtstream.WriteLine("    BACKGROUND-COLOR: white;")
txtstream.WriteLine("    FONT-FAMILY:font-family: Cambria, serif;")
txtstream.WriteLine("    FONT-SIZE: 12px;")
txtstream.WriteLine("    text-align: left;")
txtstream.WriteLine("    white-Space: nowrap;")
txtstream.WriteLine("}")
txtstream.WriteLine("td")
txtstream.WriteLine("{")
txtstream.WriteLine("    COLOR: navy;")
txtstream.WriteLine("    BACKGROUND-COLOR: white;")
txtstream.WriteLine("    FONT-FAMILY: font-family: Cambria, serif;")
txtstream.WriteLine("    FONT-SIZE: 12px;")
txtstream.WriteLine("    text-align: left;")
txtstream.WriteLine("    white-Space: nowrap;")
txtstream.WriteLine("}")
txtstream.WriteLine("</style>")
txtstream.WriteLine("</head>")
txtstream.WriteLine("<body bgcolor=""#333333" ">")
txtstream.WriteLine("<table colspacing=""3" " colpadding=""3" ">")
For each mo as ManagementObject in moc
   txtstream.WriteLine("<tr>")
   for each prop As PropertyData in mo.Properties
      txtstream.WriteLine("<th>" + prop.Name + </th>")
   next
   txtstream.WriteLine("</tr>")
   Exit For
```

Next


For each mo as ManagementObject in moc

  txtstream.WriteLine("<tr>")

  for each prop As PropertyData in mo.Properties

    txtstream.WriteLine("<td><xsl:value-of select=""data/Win32_Process/" + prop.Name + """/></td>")

  next

  txtstream.WriteLine("</tr>")

  Exit For

Next

txtstream.WriteLine("</table>")

txtstream.WriteLine("</body>")

txtstream.WriteLine("</html>")

txtstream.WriteLine("</xsl:template>")

txtstream.WriteLine("</xsl:stylesheet>")

txtstream.Close()


## For Multi Line Horizontal


Dim  ws As Object  = CreateObject("WScript.Shell")

Dim fso As Object = CreateObject("Scripting.FileSystemObject")

Dim txtstream As Object = fso.OpenTextFile(ws.CurrentDirectory + "\Process.xsl", 2, true, -2)


txtstream.WriteLine("<?xml version=""1.0" " encoding=""UTF-8" "?>")

txtstream.WriteLine("<xsl:stylesheet version=""1.0""
xmlns:xsl=""http://www.w3.org/1999/XSL/Transform" ">")

```
txtstream.WriteLine("<xsl:template match=""/""">")

txtstream.WriteLine("<html>")

txtstream.WriteLine("<head>")

txtstream.WriteLine("<title>Products</title>")

txtstream.WriteLine("<style type='text/css'>")

txtstream.WriteLine("th")

txtstream.WriteLine("{")

txtstream.WriteLine("    COLOR: darkred;")

txtstream.WriteLine("    BACKGROUND-COLOR: white;")

txtstream.WriteLine("    FONT-FAMILY:font-family: Cambria, serif;")

txtstream.WriteLine("    FONT-SIZE: 12px;")

txtstream.WriteLine("    text-align: left;")

txtstream.WriteLine("    white-Space: nowrap;")

txtstream.WriteLine("}")

txtstream.WriteLine("td")

txtstream.WriteLine("{")

txtstream.WriteLine("    COLOR: navy;")

txtstream.WriteLine("    BACKGROUND-COLOR: white;")

txtstream.WriteLine("    FONT-FAMILY: font-family: Cambria, serif;")

txtstream.WriteLine("    FONT-SIZE: 12px;")

txtstream.WriteLine("    text-align: left;")

txtstream.WriteLine("    white-Space: nowrap;")

txtstream.WriteLine("}")

txtstream.WriteLine("</style>")

txtstream.WriteLine("</head>")

txtstream.WriteLine("<body bgcolor=""#333333"" ">")

txtstream.WriteLine("<table colspacing=""3" " colpadding=""3" ">")
```

```
For each mo as ManagementObject in moc

    txtstream.WriteLine("<tr>")

    for each prop As PropertyData in mo.Properties

        txtstream.WriteLine("<th>" + prop.Name + </th>")

    next

    txtstream.WriteLine("</tr>")

    Exit For

Next

For each mo as ManagementObject in moc

    txtstream.WriteLine("<xsl:for-each select=""data/Win32_Process"">")

    txtstream.WriteLine("<tr>")

    for each prop As PropertyData in mo.Properties

        txtstream.WriteLine("<td><xsl:value-of select="" + prop.Name + """/></td>")

    next

    txtstream.WriteLine("</tr>")

    txtstream.WriteLine("</xsl:for-each>")

    Exit For

Next


txtstream.WriteLine("</table>")

txtstream.WriteLine("</body>")

txtstream.WriteLine("</html>")

txtstream.WriteLine("</xsl:template>")

txtstream.WriteLine("</xsl:stylesheet>")

txtstream.Close()
```

## For Single Line Vertical

```
Dim  ws As Object  = CreateObject("WScript.Shell")

Dim fso As Object = CreateObject("Scripting.FileSystemObject")

Dim txtstream As Object = fso.OpenTextFile(ws.CurrentDirectory + "\Process.xsl", 2, true, -2)


txtstream.WriteLine("<?xml version=""1.0" " encoding=""UTF-8" "?>")

txtstream.WriteLine("<xsl:stylesheet version=""1.0""
xmlns:xsl=""http://www.w3.org/1999/XSL/Transform" ">")

txtstream.WriteLine("<xsl:template match=""/""">")

txtstream.WriteLine("<html>")

txtstream.WriteLine("<head>")

txtstream.WriteLine("<title>Products</title>")

txtstream.WriteLine("<style type='text/css'>")

txtstream.WriteLine("th")

txtstream.WriteLine("{")

txtstream.WriteLine("    COLOR: darkred;")

txtstream.WriteLine("    BACKGROUND-COLOR: white;")

txtstream.WriteLine("    FONT-FAMILY:font-family: Cambria, serif;")

txtstream.WriteLine("    FONT-SIZE: 12px;")

txtstream.WriteLine("    text-align: left;")

txtstream.WriteLine("    white-Space: nowrap;")

txtstream.WriteLine("}")

txtstream.WriteLine("td")

txtstream.WriteLine("{")

txtstream.WriteLine("    COLOR: navy;")
```

```
txtstream.WriteLine("    BACKGROUND-COLOR: white;")

txtstream.WriteLine("    FONT-FAMILY: font-family: Cambria, serif;")

txtstream.WriteLine("    FONT-SIZE: 12px;")

txtstream.WriteLine("    text-align: left;")

txtstream.WriteLine("    white-Space: nowrap;")

txtstream.WriteLine("}")

txtstream.WriteLine("</style>")

txtstream.WriteLine("</head>")

txtstream.WriteLine("<body bgcolor=""#333333" ">")

txtstream.WriteLine("<table colspacing=""3" " colpadding=""3" ">")

For each mo as ManagementObject in moc

   For each prop As PropertyData in mo.Properties

      txtstream.WriteLine("<tr><th>" + prop.Name + </th>")

      txtstream.WriteLine("<td><xsl:value-of select=""data/Win32_Process/" +
prop.Name + """/></td></tr>")

   next

   Exit For

Next

txtstream.WriteLine("</table>")

txtstream.WriteLine("</body>")

txtstream.WriteLine("</html>")

txtstream.WriteLine("</xsl:template>")

txtstream.WriteLine("</xsl:stylesheet>")

txtstream.Close()
```

For Multi Line Vertical

```
Dim  ws As Object  = CreateObject("WScript.Shell")

Dim fso As Object = CreateObject("Scripting.FileSystemObject")

Dim txtstream As Object = fso.OpenTextFile(ws.CurrentDirectory + "\Process.xsl", 2,
true, -2)


txtstream.WriteLine("<?xml version=""1.0"" " encoding=""UTF-8" "?>")

txtstream.WriteLine("<xsl:stylesheet version=""1.0""
xmlns:xsl=""http://www.w3.org/1999/XSL/Transform" ">")

txtstream.WriteLine("<xsl:template match=""/"">")

txtstream.WriteLine("<html>")

txtstream.WriteLine("<head>")

txtstream.WriteLine("<title>Products</title>")

txtstream.WriteLine("<style type='text/css'>")

txtstream.WriteLine("th")

txtstream.WriteLine("{")

txtstream.WriteLine("   COLOR: darkred;")

txtstream.WriteLine("   BACKGROUND-COLOR: white;")

txtstream.WriteLine("   FONT-FAMILY:font-family: Cambria, serif;")

txtstream.WriteLine("   FONT-SIZE: 12px;")

txtstream.WriteLine("   text-align: left;")

txtstream.WriteLine("   white-Space: nowrap;")

txtstream.WriteLine("}")

txtstream.WriteLine("td")

txtstream.WriteLine("{")

txtstream.WriteLine("   COLOR: navy;")

txtstream.WriteLine("   BACKGROUND-COLOR: white;")

txtstream.WriteLine("   FONT-FAMILY: font-family: Cambria, serif;")

txtstream.WriteLine("   FONT-SIZE: 12px;")
```

```
txtstream.WriteLine("    text-align: left;")
txtstream.WriteLine("    white-Space: nowrap;")
txtstream.WriteLine("}")
txtstream.WriteLine("</style>")
txtstream.WriteLine("</head>")
txtstream.WriteLine("<body bgcolor=""#333333" ">")
txtstream.WriteLine("<table colspacing=""3" " colpadding=""3" ">")
txtstream.WriteLine("<tr>")
For each mo as ManagementObject in moc
   for each prop As PropertyData in mo.Properties
      txtstream.WriteLine("<tr><th>" + prop.Name + </th>")
      txtstream.WriteLine("<td><xsl:for-each select=""data/Win32_Process"">")
      txtstream.WriteLine("<xsl:value-of select="""" + prop.Name + """/></td>")
      txtstream.WriteLine("</xsl:for-each></tr>")
   next
   Exit For
Next
txtstream.WriteLine("</table>")
txtstream.WriteLine("</body>")
txtstream.WriteLine("</html>")
txtstream.WriteLine("</xsl:template>")
txtstream.WriteLine("</xsl:stylesheet>")
txtstream.Close()
```

System.Management.ManagementClass Code

```
Dim cops As ConnectionOptions = New ConnectionOptions()
cops.Authentication = AuthenticationLevel.PacketPrivacy
cops.Impersonation = ImpersonationLevel.Impersonate
cops.Locale = "MS-0409"

Dim path As ManagementPath = New ManagementPath()
path.NamespacePath = "root\cimv2"
path.ClassName = "Win32_Process"
path.Server = "LocalHost"


Dim scope As ManagementScope = New ManagementScope(path, cops)
scope.Connect()

Dim mc As ManagementClass = New ManagementClass()
mc.Path = scope.Path
mc.Scope = scope

Dim moc As ManagementObjectCollection = mc.GetInstances()
```

Function GetManagementValue(ByVal Name As String, ByVal mo As ManagementObject)

```
Dim tempstr, pos, pName
pName = vbTab & Name & " = "
tempstr = mo.GetText(TextFormat.Mof)
pos = InStr(tempstr, Name)
If pos > 0 Then
  pos = pos + Len(Name) + 2
  tempstr = Mid(tempstr, pos, Len(tempstr))
  pos = InStr(tempstr, ";")
  tempstr = Mid(tempstr, 1, pos - 1)
  tempstr = Replace(tempstr, Chr(34), "")
  tempstr = Replace(tempstr, "{", "")
  tempstr = Replace(tempstr, "}", "")
  tempstr = Trim(tempstr)
  If Len(tempstr) > 13 Then
    If mo.Properties.Item(Name).Type = CimType.DateTime Then
      tempstr = Mid(tempstr, 5, 2) + "/" + _
          Mid(tempstr, 7, 2) + "/" + _
          Mid(tempstr, 1, 4) + " " + _
          Mid(tempstr, 9, 2) + ":" + _
          Mid(tempstr, 11, 2) + ":" + _
          Mid(tempstr, 13, 2)

    End If

  End If
  GetManagementValue = tempstr

Else

  GetManagementValue = ""
```

```
        End If

    End Function
```

# Stylesheets

## *Decorating your web pages*

BELOW ARE SOME STYLESHEETS I COOKED UP THAT I LIKE AND THINK YOU MIGHT TOO. Don't worry I won't be offended if you take and modify to your hearts delight. Please do!

NONE

```
txtstream.WriteLine("<style type='text/css'>")

txtstream.WriteLine("th")

txtstream.WriteLine("{")

txtstream.WriteLine("    COLOR: white;")

txtstream.WriteLine("}")

txtstream.WriteLine("td")

txtstream.WriteLine("{")

txtstream.WriteLine("    COLOR: white;")

txtstream.WriteLine("}")
```

```
txtstream.WriteLine("</style>")
```

BLACK AND WHITE TEXT

```
txtstream.WriteLine("<style type='text/css'>")
txtstream.WriteLine("th")
txtstream.WriteLine("{")
txtstream.WriteLine("   COLOR: white;")
txtstream.WriteLine("   BACKGROUND-COLOR: black;")
txtstream.WriteLine("   FONT-FAMILY:font-family: Cambria, serif;")
txtstream.WriteLine("   FONT-SIZE: 12px;")
txtstream.WriteLine("   text-align: left;")
txtstream.WriteLine("   white-Space: nowrap;")
txtstream.WriteLine("}")
txtstream.WriteLine("td")
txtstream.WriteLine("{")
txtstream.WriteLine("   COLOR: white;")
txtstream.WriteLine("   BACKGROUND-COLOR: black;")
txtstream.WriteLine("   FONT-FAMILY: font-family: Cambria, serif;")
txtstream.WriteLine("   FONT-SIZE: 12px;")
txtstream.WriteLine("   text-align: left;")
txtstream.WriteLine("   white-Space: nowrap;")
txtstream.WriteLine("}")
txtstream.WriteLine("div")
txtstream.WriteLine("{")
txtstream.WriteLine("   COLOR: white;")
txtstream.WriteLine("   BACKGROUND-COLOR: black;")
```

```
txtstream.WriteLine("   FONT-FAMILY: font-family: Cambria, serif;")
txtstream.WriteLine("   FONT-SIZE: 10px;")
txtstream.WriteLine("   text-align: left;")
txtstream.WriteLine("   white-Space: nowrap;")
txtstream.WriteLine("}")
txtstream.WriteLine("span")
txtstream.WriteLine("{")
txtstream.WriteLine("   COLOR: white;")
txtstream.WriteLine("   BACKGROUND-COLOR: black;")
txtstream.WriteLine("   FONT-FAMILY: font-family: Cambria, serif;")
txtstream.WriteLine("   FONT-SIZE: 10px;")
txtstream.WriteLine("   text-align: left;")
txtstream.WriteLine("   white-Space: nowrap;")
txtstream.WriteLine("   display:inline-block;")
txtstream.WriteLine("   width: 100%;")
txtstream.WriteLine("}")
txtstream.WriteLine("textarea")
txtstream.WriteLine("{")
txtstream.WriteLine("   COLOR: white;")
txtstream.WriteLine("   BACKGROUND-COLOR: black;")
txtstream.WriteLine("   FONT-FAMILY: font-family: Cambria, serif;")
txtstream.WriteLine("   FONT-SIZE: 10px;")
txtstream.WriteLine("   text-align: left;")
txtstream.WriteLine("   white-Space: nowrap;")
txtstream.WriteLine("   width: 100%;")
txtstream.WriteLine("}")
txtstream.WriteLine("select")
```

```
txtstream.WriteLine("{")

txtstream.WriteLine("    COLOR: white;")

txtstream.WriteLine("    BACKGROUND-COLOR: black;")

txtstream.WriteLine("    FONT-FAMILY: font-family: Cambria, serif;")

txtstream.WriteLine("    FONT-SIZE: 10px;")

txtstream.WriteLine("    text-align: left;")

txtstream.WriteLine("    white-Space: nowrap;")

txtstream.WriteLine("    width: 100%;")

txtstream.WriteLine("}")

txtstream.WriteLine("input")

txtstream.WriteLine("{")

txtstream.WriteLine("    COLOR: white;")

txtstream.WriteLine("    BACKGROUND-COLOR: black;")

txtstream.WriteLine("    FONT-FAMILY: font-family: Cambria, serif;")

txtstream.WriteLine("    FONT-SIZE: 12px;")

txtstream.WriteLine("    text-align: left;")

txtstream.WriteLine("    display:table-cell;")

txtstream.WriteLine("    white-Space: nowrap;")

txtstream.WriteLine("}")

txtstream.WriteLine("h1 {")

txtstream.WriteLine("color: antiquewhite;")

txtstream.WriteLine("text-shadow: 1px 1px black;")

txtstream.WriteLine("padding: 3px;")

txtstream.WriteLine("text-align: center;")

txtstream.WriteLine("box-shadow: inset 2px 5px rgba(0,0,0,0.5), inset -2px -2px 5px rgba(255,255,255,0.5);")

txtstream.WriteLine("}")
```

```
txtstream.WriteLine("</style>")
```

COLORED TEXT

```
txtstream.WriteLine("<style type='text/css'>")
txtstream.WriteLine("th")
txtstream.WriteLine("{")
txtstream.WriteLine("   COLOR: darkred;")
txtstream.WriteLine("   BACKGROUND-COLOR: #eeeeee;")
txtstream.WriteLine("   FONT-FAMILY:font-family: Cambria, serif;")
txtstream.WriteLine("   FONT-SIZE: 12px;")
txtstream.WriteLine("   text-align: left;")
txtstream.WriteLine("   white-Space: nowrap;")
txtstream.WriteLine("}")
txtstream.WriteLine("td")
txtstream.WriteLine("{")
txtstream.WriteLine("   COLOR: navy;")
txtstream.WriteLine("   BACKGROUND-COLOR: #eeeeee;")
txtstream.WriteLine("   FONT-FAMILY: font-family: Cambria, serif;")
txtstream.WriteLine("   FONT-SIZE: 12px;")
txtstream.WriteLine("   text-align: left;")
txtstream.WriteLine("   white-Space: nowrap;")
txtstream.WriteLine("}")
txtstream.WriteLine("div")
txtstream.WriteLine("{")
txtstream.WriteLine("   COLOR: white;")
txtstream.WriteLine("   BACKGROUND-COLOR: navy;")
```

```
txtstream.WriteLine("   FONT-FAMILY: font-family: Cambria, serif;")
txtstream.WriteLine("   FONT-SIZE: 10px;")
txtstream.WriteLine("   text-align: left;")
txtstream.WriteLine("   white-Space: nowrap;")
txtstream.WriteLine("}")
txtstream.WriteLine("span")
txtstream.WriteLine("{")
txtstream.WriteLine("   COLOR: white;")
txtstream.WriteLine("   BACKGROUND-COLOR: navy;")
txtstream.WriteLine("   FONT-FAMILY: font-family: Cambria, serif;")
txtstream.WriteLine("   FONT-SIZE: 10px;")
txtstream.WriteLine("   text-align: left;")
txtstream.WriteLine("   white-Space: nowrap;")
txtstream.WriteLine("   display:inline-block;")
txtstream.WriteLine("   width: 100%;")
txtstream.WriteLine("}")
txtstream.WriteLine("textarea")
txtstream.WriteLine("{")
txtstream.WriteLine("   COLOR: white;")
txtstream.WriteLine("   BACKGROUND-COLOR: navy;")
txtstream.WriteLine("   FONT-FAMILY: font-family: Cambria, serif;")
txtstream.WriteLine("   FONT-SIZE: 10px;")
txtstream.WriteLine("   text-align: left;")
txtstream.WriteLine("   white-Space: nowrap;")
txtstream.WriteLine("   width: 100%;")
txtstream.WriteLine("}")
txtstream.WriteLine("select")
```

```
txtstream.WriteLine("{")

txtstream.WriteLine("   COLOR: white;")

txtstream.WriteLine("   BACKGROUND-COLOR: navy;")

txtstream.WriteLine("   FONT-FAMILY: font-family: Cambria, serif;")

txtstream.WriteLine("   FONT-SIZE: 10px;")

txtstream.WriteLine("   text-align: left;")

txtstream.WriteLine("   white-Space: nowrap;")

txtstream.WriteLine("   width: 100%;")

txtstream.WriteLine("}")

txtstream.WriteLine("input")

txtstream.WriteLine("{")

txtstream.WriteLine("   COLOR: white;")

txtstream.WriteLine("   BACKGROUND-COLOR: navy;")

txtstream.WriteLine("   FONT-FAMILY: font-family: Cambria, serif;")

txtstream.WriteLine("   FONT-SIZE: 12px;")

txtstream.WriteLine("   text-align: left;")

txtstream.WriteLine("   display:table-cell;")

txtstream.WriteLine("   white-Space: nowrap;")

txtstream.WriteLine("}")

txtstream.WriteLine("h1 {")

txtstream.WriteLine("color: antiquewhite;")

txtstream.WriteLine("text-shadow: 1px 1px black;")

txtstream.WriteLine("padding: 3px;")

txtstream.WriteLine("text-align: center;")

txtstream.WriteLine("box-shadow: inset 2px 5px rgba(0,0,0,0.5), inset -2px -2px
5px rgba(255,255,255,0.5);")

txtstream.WriteLine("}")
```

```
txtstream.WriteLine("</style>")
```

OSCILLATING ROW COLORS

```
txtstream.WriteLine("<style>")
txtstream.WriteLine("th")
txtstream.WriteLine("{")
txtstream.WriteLine("    COLOR: white;")
txtstream.WriteLine("    BACKGROUND-COLOR: navy;")
txtstream.WriteLine("    FONT-FAMILY:font-family: Cambria, serif;")
txtstream.WriteLine("    FONT-SIZE: 12px;")
txtstream.WriteLine("    text-align: left;")
txtstream.WriteLine("    white-Space: nowrap;")
txtstream.WriteLine("}")
txtstream.WriteLine("td")
txtstream.WriteLine("{")
txtstream.WriteLine("    COLOR: navy;")
txtstream.WriteLine("    FONT-FAMILY: font-family: Cambria, serif;")
txtstream.WriteLine("    FONT-SIZE: 12px;")
txtstream.WriteLine("    text-align: left;")
txtstream.WriteLine("    white-Space: nowrap;")
txtstream.WriteLine("}")
txtstream.WriteLine("div")
txtstream.WriteLine("{")
txtstream.WriteLine("    COLOR: navy;")
```

```
txtstream.WriteLine("    FONT-FAMILY: font-family: Cambria, serif;")
txtstream.WriteLine("    FONT-SIZE: 12px;")
txtstream.WriteLine("    text-align: left;")
txtstream.WriteLine("    white-Space: nowrap;")
txtstream.WriteLine("}")
txtstream.WriteLine("span")
txtstream.WriteLine("{")
txtstream.WriteLine("    COLOR: navy;")
txtstream.WriteLine("    FONT-FAMILY: font-family: Cambria, serif;")
txtstream.WriteLine("    FONT-SIZE: 12px;")
txtstream.WriteLine("    text-align: left;")
txtstream.WriteLine("    white-Space: nowrap;")
txtstream.WriteLine("    width: 100%;")
txtstream.WriteLine("}")
txtstream.WriteLine("textarea")
txtstream.WriteLine("{")
txtstream.WriteLine("    COLOR: navy;")
txtstream.WriteLine("    FONT-FAMILY: font-family: Cambria, serif;")
txtstream.WriteLine("    FONT-SIZE: 12px;")
txtstream.WriteLine("    text-align: left;")
txtstream.WriteLine("    white-Space: nowrap;")
txtstream.WriteLine("    display:inline-block;")
txtstream.WriteLine("    width: 100%;")
txtstream.WriteLine("}")
txtstream.WriteLine("select")
txtstream.WriteLine("{")
txtstream.WriteLine("    COLOR: navy;")
```

```
txtstream.WriteLine("   FONT-FAMILY: font-family: Cambria, serif;")
txtstream.WriteLine("   FONT-SIZE: 10px;")
txtstream.WriteLine("   text-align: left;")
txtstream.WriteLine("   white-Space: nowrap;")
txtstream.WriteLine("   display:inline-block;")
txtstream.WriteLine("   width: 100%;")
txtstream.WriteLine("}")
txtstream.WriteLine("input")
txtstream.WriteLine("{")
txtstream.WriteLine("   COLOR: navy;")
txtstream.WriteLine("   FONT-FAMILY: font-family: Cambria, serif;")
txtstream.WriteLine("   FONT-SIZE: 12px;")
txtstream.WriteLine("   text-align: left;")
txtstream.WriteLine("   display:table-cell;")
txtstream.WriteLine("   white-Space: nowrap;")
txtstream.WriteLine("}")
txtstream.WriteLine("h1 {")
txtstream.WriteLine("color: antiquewhite;")
txtstream.WriteLine("text-shadow: 1px black;")
txtstream.WriteLine("padding: 3px;")
txtstream.WriteLine("text-align: center;")
txtstream.WriteLine("box-shadow: inset 2px 5px rgba(0,0,0,0.5), inset -2px -2px 5px rgba(255,255,255,0.5);")
txtstream.WriteLine("}")
txtstream.WriteLine("tr:nth-child(even){background-color:#f2f2f2;}")
txtstream.WriteLine("tr:nth-child(odd){background-color:#cccccc; color:#f2f2f2;}")
txtstream.WriteLine("</style>")
```

GHOST DECORATED

txtstream.WriteLine("<style type='text/css'>")

txtstream.WriteLine("th")

txtstream.WriteLine("{")

txtstream.WriteLine("    COLOR: black;")

txtstream.WriteLine("    BACKGROUND-COLOR: white;")

txtstream.WriteLine("    FONT-FAMILY:font-family: Cambria, serif;")

txtstream.WriteLine("    FONT-SIZE: 12px;")

txtstream.WriteLine("    text-align: left;")

txtstream.WriteLine("    white-Space: nowrap;")

txtstream.WriteLine("}")

txtstream.WriteLine("td")

txtstream.WriteLine("{")

txtstream.WriteLine("    COLOR: black;")

txtstream.WriteLine("    BACKGROUND-COLOR: white;")

txtstream.WriteLine("    FONT-FAMILY: font-family: Cambria, serif;")

txtstream.WriteLine("    FONT-SIZE: 12px;")

txtstream.WriteLine("    text-align: left;")

txtstream.WriteLine("    white-Space: nowrap;")

txtstream.WriteLine("}")

txtstream.WriteLine("div")

txtstream.WriteLine("{")

txtstream.WriteLine("    COLOR: black;")

txtstream.WriteLine("    BACKGROUND-COLOR: white;")

txtstream.WriteLine("    FONT-FAMILY: font-family: Cambria, serif;")

```
txtstream.WriteLine("    FONT-SIZE: 10px;")
txtstream.WriteLine("    text-align: left;")
txtstream.WriteLine("    white-Space: nowrap;")
txtstream.WriteLine("}")
txtstream.WriteLine("span")
txtstream.WriteLine("{")
txtstream.WriteLine("    COLOR: black;")
txtstream.WriteLine("    BACKGROUND-COLOR: white;")
txtstream.WriteLine("    FONT-FAMILY: font-family: Cambria, serif;")
txtstream.WriteLine("    FONT-SIZE: 10px;")
txtstream.WriteLine("    text-align: left;")
txtstream.WriteLine("    white-Space: nowrap;")
txtstream.WriteLine("    display:inline-block;")
txtstream.WriteLine("    width: 100%;")
txtstream.WriteLine("}")
txtstream.WriteLine("textarea")
txtstream.WriteLine("{")
txtstream.WriteLine("    COLOR: black;")
txtstream.WriteLine("    BACKGROUND-COLOR: white;")
txtstream.WriteLine("    FONT-FAMILY: font-family: Cambria, serif;")
txtstream.WriteLine("    FONT-SIZE: 10px;")
txtstream.WriteLine("    text-align: left;")
txtstream.WriteLine("    white-Space: nowrap;")
txtstream.WriteLine("    width: 100%;")
txtstream.WriteLine("}")
txtstream.WriteLine("select")
txtstream.WriteLine("{")
```

```
txtstream.WriteLine("    COLOR: black;")
txtstream.WriteLine("    BACKGROUND-COLOR: white;")
txtstream.WriteLine("    FONT-FAMILY: font-family: Cambria, serif;")
txtstream.WriteLine("    FONT-SIZE: 10px;")
txtstream.WriteLine("    text-align: left;")
txtstream.WriteLine("    white-Space: nowrap;")
txtstream.WriteLine("    width: 100%;")
txtstream.WriteLine("}")
txtstream.WriteLine("input")
txtstream.WriteLine("{")
txtstream.WriteLine("    COLOR: black;")
txtstream.WriteLine("    BACKGROUND-COLOR: white;")
txtstream.WriteLine("    FONT-FAMILY: font-family: Cambria, serif;")
txtstream.WriteLine("    FONT-SIZE: 12px;")
txtstream.WriteLine("    text-align: left;")
txtstream.WriteLine("    display:table-cell;")
txtstream.WriteLine("    white-Space: nowrap;")
txtstream.WriteLine("}")
txtstream.WriteLine("h1 {")
txtstream.WriteLine("color: antiquewhite;")
txtstream.WriteLine("text-shadow: 1px black;")
txtstream.WriteLine("padding: 3px;")
txtstream.WriteLine("text-align: center;")
txtstream.WriteLine("box-shadow: inset 2px 5px rgba(0,0,0,0.5), inset -2px -2px 5px rgba(255,255,255,0.5);")
txtstream.WriteLine("}")
txtstream.WriteLine("</style>")
```

```
txtstream.WriteLine("<style type='text/css'>")

txtstream.WriteLine("body")

txtstream.WriteLine("{")

txtstream.WriteLine("   PADDING-RIGHT: 0px;")

txtstream.WriteLine("   PADDING-LEFT: 0px;")

txtstream.WriteLine("   PADDING-BOTTOM: 0px;")

txtstream.WriteLine("   MARGIN: 0px;")

txtstream.WriteLine("   COLOR: #333;")

txtstream.WriteLine("   PADDING-TOP: 0px;")

txtstream.WriteLine("   FONT-FAMILY: verdana, arial, helvetica, sans-serif;")

txtstream.WriteLine("}")

txtstream.WriteLine("table")

txtstream.WriteLine("{")

txtstream.WriteLine("   BORDER-RIGHT: #999999 3px solid;")

txtstream.WriteLine("   PADDING-RIGHT: 6px;")

txtstream.WriteLine("   PADDING-LEFT: 6px;")

txtstream.WriteLine("   FONT-WEIGHT: Bold;")

txtstream.WriteLine("   FONT-SIZE: 14px;")

txtstream.WriteLine("   PADDING-BOTTOM: 6px;")

txtstream.WriteLine("   COLOR: Peru;")

txtstream.WriteLine("   LINE-HEIGHT: 14px;")

txtstream.WriteLine("   PADDING-TOP: 6px;")

txtstream.WriteLine("   BORDER-BOTTOM: #999 1px solid;")
```

```
txtstream.WriteLine("   BACKGROUND-COLOR: #eeeeee;")
txtstream.WriteLine("   FONT-FAMILY: verdana, arial, helvetica, sans-serif;")
txtstream.WriteLine("   FONT-SIZE: 12px;")
txtstream.WriteLine("}")
txtstream.WriteLine("th")
txtstream.WriteLine("{")
txtstream.WriteLine("   BORDER-RIGHT: #999999 3px solid;")
txtstream.WriteLine("   PADDING-RIGHT: 6px;")
txtstream.WriteLine("   PADDING-LEFT: 6px;")
txtstream.WriteLine("   FONT-WEIGHT: Bold;")
txtstream.WriteLine("   FONT-SIZE: 14px;")
txtstream.WriteLine("   PADDING-BOTTOM: 6px;")
txtstream.WriteLine("   COLOR: darkred;")
txtstream.WriteLine("   LINE-HEIGHT: 14px;")
txtstream.WriteLine("   PADDING-TOP: 6px;")
txtstream.WriteLine("   BORDER-BOTTOM: #999 1px solid;")
txtstream.WriteLine("   BACKGROUND-COLOR: #eeeeee;")
txtstream.WriteLine("   FONT-FAMILY:font-family: Cambria, serif;")
txtstream.WriteLine("   FONT-SIZE: 12px;")
txtstream.WriteLine("   text-align: left;")
txtstream.WriteLine("   white-Space: nowrap;")
txtstream.WriteLine("}")
txtstream.WriteLine(".th")
txtstream.WriteLine("{")
txtstream.WriteLine("   BORDER-RIGHT: #999999 2px solid;")
txtstream.WriteLine("   PADDING-RIGHT: 6px;")
txtstream.WriteLine("   PADDING-LEFT: 6px;")
```

```
txtstream.WriteLine("    FONT-WEIGHT: Bold;")
txtstream.WriteLine("    PADDING-BOTTOM: 6px;")
txtstream.WriteLine("    COLOR: black;")
txtstream.WriteLine("    PADDING-TOP: 6px;")
txtstream.WriteLine("    BORDER-BOTTOM: #999 2px solid;")
txtstream.WriteLine("    BACKGROUND-COLOR: #eeeeee;")
txtstream.WriteLine("    FONT-FAMILY: font-family: Cambria, serif;")
txtstream.WriteLine("    FONT-SIZE: 10px;")
txtstream.WriteLine("    text-align: right;")
txtstream.WriteLine("    white-Space: nowrap;")
txtstream.WriteLine("}")
txtstream.WriteLine("td")
txtstream.WriteLine("{")
txtstream.WriteLine("    BORDER-RIGHT: #999999 3px solid;")
txtstream.WriteLine("    PADDING-RIGHT: 6px;")
txtstream.WriteLine("    PADDING-LEFT: 6px;")
txtstream.WriteLine("    FONT-WEIGHT: Normal;")
txtstream.WriteLine("    PADDING-BOTTOM: 6px;")
txtstream.WriteLine("    COLOR: navy;")
txtstream.WriteLine("    LINE-HEIGHT: 14px;")
txtstream.WriteLine("    PADDING-TOP: 6px;")
txtstream.WriteLine("    BORDER-BOTTOM: #999 1px solid;")
txtstream.WriteLine("    BACKGROUND-COLOR: #eeeeee;")
txtstream.WriteLine("    FONT-FAMILY: font-family: Cambria, serif;")
txtstream.WriteLine("    FONT-SIZE: 12px;")
txtstream.WriteLine("    text-align: left;")
txtstream.WriteLine("    white-Space: nowrap;")
```

txtstream.WriteLine("}")

txtstream.WriteLine("div")

txtstream.WriteLine("{")

txtstream.WriteLine("    BORDER-RIGHT: #999999 3px solid;")

txtstream.WriteLine("    PADDING-RIGHT: 6px;")

txtstream.WriteLine("    PADDING-LEFT: 6px;")

txtstream.WriteLine("    FONT-WEIGHT: Normal;")

txtstream.WriteLine("    PADDING-BOTTOM: 6px;")

txtstream.WriteLine("    COLOR: white;")

txtstream.WriteLine("    PADDING-TOP: 6px;")

txtstream.WriteLine("    BORDER-BOTTOM: #999 1px solid;")

txtstream.WriteLine("    BACKGROUND-COLOR: navy;")

txtstream.WriteLine("    FONT-FAMILY: font-family: Cambria, serif;")

txtstream.WriteLine("    FONT-SIZE: 10px;")

txtstream.WriteLine("    text-align: left;")

txtstream.WriteLine("    white-Space: nowrap;")

txtstream.WriteLine("}")

txtstream.WriteLine("span")

txtstream.WriteLine("{")

txtstream.WriteLine("    BORDER-RIGHT: #999999 3px solid;")

txtstream.WriteLine("    PADDING-RIGHT: 3px;")

txtstream.WriteLine("    PADDING-LEFT: 3px;")

txtstream.WriteLine("    FONT-WEIGHT: Normal;")

txtstream.WriteLine("    PADDING-BOTTOM: 3px;")

txtstream.WriteLine("    COLOR: white;")

txtstream.WriteLine("    PADDING-TOP: 3px;")

txtstream.WriteLine("    BORDER-BOTTOM: #999 1px solid;")

```
txtstream.WriteLine("    BACKGROUND-COLOR: navy;")
txtstream.WriteLine("    FONT-FAMILY: font-family: Cambria, serif;")
txtstream.WriteLine("    FONT-SIZE: 10px;")
txtstream.WriteLine("    text-align: left;")
txtstream.WriteLine("    white-Space: nowrap;")
txtstream.WriteLine("    display:inline-block;")
txtstream.WriteLine("    width: 100%;")
txtstream.WriteLine("}")
txtstream.WriteLine("textarea")
txtstream.WriteLine("{")
txtstream.WriteLine("    BORDER-RIGHT: #999999 3px solid;")
txtstream.WriteLine("    PADDING-RIGHT: 3px;")
txtstream.WriteLine("    PADDING-LEFT: 3px;")
txtstream.WriteLine("    FONT-WEIGHT: Normal;")
txtstream.WriteLine("    PADDING-BOTTOM: 3px;")
txtstream.WriteLine("    COLOR: white;")
txtstream.WriteLine("    PADDING-TOP: 3px;")
txtstream.WriteLine("    BORDER-BOTTOM: #999 1px solid;")
txtstream.WriteLine("    BACKGROUND-COLOR: navy;")
txtstream.WriteLine("    FONT-FAMILY: font-family: Cambria, serif;")
txtstream.WriteLine("    FONT-SIZE: 10px;")
txtstream.WriteLine("    text-align: left;")
txtstream.WriteLine("    white-Space: nowrap;")
txtstream.WriteLine("    width: 100%;")
txtstream.WriteLine("}")
txtstream.WriteLine("select")
txtstream.WriteLine("{")
```

```
txtstream.WriteLine("   BORDER-RIGHT: #999999 3px solid;")
txtstream.WriteLine("   PADDING-RIGHT: 6px;")
txtstream.WriteLine("   PADDING-LEFT: 6px;")
txtstream.WriteLine("   FONT-WEIGHT: Normal;")
txtstream.WriteLine("   PADDING-BOTTOM: 6px;")
txtstream.WriteLine("   COLOR: white;")
txtstream.WriteLine("   PADDING-TOP: 6px;")
txtstream.WriteLine("   BORDER-BOTTOM: #999 1px solid;")
txtstream.WriteLine("   BACKGROUND-COLOR: navy;")
txtstream.WriteLine("   FONT-FAMILY: font-family: Cambria, serif;")
txtstream.WriteLine("   FONT-SIZE: 10px;")
txtstream.WriteLine("   text-align: left;")
txtstream.WriteLine("   white-Space: nowrap;")
txtstream.WriteLine("   width: 100%;")
txtstream.WriteLine("}")
txtstream.WriteLine("input")
txtstream.WriteLine("{")
txtstream.WriteLine("   BORDER-RIGHT: #999999 3px solid;")
txtstream.WriteLine("   PADDING-RIGHT: 3px;")
txtstream.WriteLine("   PADDING-LEFT: 3px;")
txtstream.WriteLine("   FONT-WEIGHT: Bold;")
txtstream.WriteLine("   PADDING-BOTTOM: 3px;")
txtstream.WriteLine("   COLOR: white;")
txtstream.WriteLine("   PADDING-TOP: 3px;")
txtstream.WriteLine("   BORDER-BOTTOM: #999 1px solid;")
txtstream.WriteLine("   BACKGROUND-COLOR: navy;")
txtstream.WriteLine("   FONT-FAMILY: font-family: Cambria, serif;")
```

```
txtstream.WriteLine("    FONT-SIZE: 12px;")

txtstream.WriteLine("    text-align: left;")

txtstream.WriteLine("    display:table-cell;")

txtstream.WriteLine("    white-Space: nowrap;")

txtstream.WriteLine("    width: 100%;")

txtstream.WriteLine("}")

txtstream.WriteLine("h1 {")

txtstream.WriteLine("color: antiquewhite;")

txtstream.WriteLine("text-shadow: 1px 1px black;")

txtstream.WriteLine("padding: 3px;")

txtstream.WriteLine("text-align: center;")

txtstream.WriteLine("box-shadow: inset 2px 5px rgba(0,0,0,0.5), inset -2px -2px 5px rgba(255,255,255,0.5);")

txtstream.WriteLine("}")

txtstream.WriteLine("</style>")
```

## SHADOW BOX

```
txtstream.WriteLine("<style type='text/css'>")

txtstream.WriteLine("body")

txtstream.WriteLine("{")

txtstream.WriteLine("    PADDING-RIGHT: 0px;")

txtstream.WriteLine("    PADDING-LEFT: 0px;")

txtstream.WriteLine("    PADDING-BOTTOM: 0px;")

txtstream.WriteLine("    MARGIN: 0px;")

txtstream.WriteLine("    COLOR: #333;")

txtstream.WriteLine("    PADDING-TOP: 0px;")
```

```
txtstream.WriteLine("    FONT-FAMILY: verdana, arial, helvetica, sans-serif;")

txtstream.WriteLine("}")

txtstream.WriteLine("table")

txtstream.WriteLine("{")

txtstream.WriteLine("    BORDER-RIGHT: #999999 1px solid;")

txtstream.WriteLine("    PADDING-RIGHT: 1px;")

txtstream.WriteLine("    PADDING-LEFT: 1px;")

txtstream.WriteLine("    PADDING-BOTTOM: 1px;")

txtstream.WriteLine("    LINE-HEIGHT: 8px;")

txtstream.WriteLine("    PADDING-TOP: 1px;")

txtstream.WriteLine("    BORDER-BOTTOM: #999 1px solid;")

txtstream.WriteLine("    BACKGROUND-COLOR: #eeeeee;")

txtstream.WriteLine("    filter:progid:DXImageTransform.Microsoft.Shadow(color='silver', Direction=135, Strength=16")

txtstream.WriteLine("}")

txtstream.WriteLine("th")

txtstream.WriteLine("{")

txtstream.WriteLine("    BORDER-RIGHT: #999999 3px solid;")

txtstream.WriteLine("    PADDING-RIGHT: 6px;")

txtstream.WriteLine("    PADDING-LEFT: 6px;")

txtstream.WriteLine("    FONT-WEIGHT: Bold;")

txtstream.WriteLine("    FONT-SIZE: 14px;")

txtstream.WriteLine("    PADDING-BOTTOM: 6px;")

txtstream.WriteLine("    COLOR: darkred;")

txtstream.WriteLine("    LINE-HEIGHT: 14px;")

txtstream.WriteLine("    PADDING-TOP: 6px;")

txtstream.WriteLine("    BORDER-BOTTOM: #999 1px solid;")
```

```
txtstream.WriteLine("    BACKGROUND-COLOR: #eeeeee;")
txtstream.WriteLine("    FONT-FAMILY: font-family: Cambria, serif;")
txtstream.WriteLine("    FONT-SIZE: 12px;")
txtstream.WriteLine("    text-align: left;")
txtstream.WriteLine("    white-Space: nowrap;")
txtstream.WriteLine("}")
txtstream.WriteLine(".th")
txtstream.WriteLine("{")
txtstream.WriteLine("    BORDER-RIGHT: #999999 2px solid;")
txtstream.WriteLine("    PADDING-RIGHT: 6px;")
txtstream.WriteLine("    PADDING-LEFT: 6px;")
txtstream.WriteLine("    FONT-WEIGHT: Bold;")
txtstream.WriteLine("    PADDING-BOTTOM: 6px;")
txtstream.WriteLine("    COLOR: black;")
txtstream.WriteLine("    PADDING-TOP: 6px;")
txtstream.WriteLine("    BORDER-BOTTOM: #999 2px solid;")
txtstream.WriteLine("    BACKGROUND-COLOR: #eeeeee;")
txtstream.WriteLine("    FONT-FAMILY: font-family: Cambria, serif;")
txtstream.WriteLine("    FONT-SIZE: 10px;")
txtstream.WriteLine("    text-align: right;")
txtstream.WriteLine("    white-Space: nowrap;")
txtstream.WriteLine("}")
txtstream.WriteLine("td")
txtstream.WriteLine("{")
txtstream.WriteLine("    BORDER-RIGHT: #999999 3px solid;")
txtstream.WriteLine("    PADDING-RIGHT: 6px;")
txtstream.WriteLine("    PADDING-LEFT: 6px;")
```

```
txtstream.WriteLine("    FONT-WEIGHT: Normal;")
txtstream.WriteLine("    PADDING-BOTTOM: 6px;")
txtstream.WriteLine("    COLOR: navy;")
txtstream.WriteLine("    LINE-HEIGHT: 14px;")
txtstream.WriteLine("    PADDING-TOP: 6px;")
txtstream.WriteLine("    BORDER-BOTTOM: #999 1px solid;")
txtstream.WriteLine("    BACKGROUND-COLOR: #eeeeee;")
txtstream.WriteLine("    FONT-FAMILY: font-family: Cambria, serif;")
txtstream.WriteLine("    FONT-SIZE: 12px;")
txtstream.WriteLine("    text-align: left;")
txtstream.WriteLine("    white-Space: nowrap;")
txtstream.WriteLine("}")
txtstream.WriteLine("div")
txtstream.WriteLine("{")
txtstream.WriteLine("    BORDER-RIGHT: #999999 3px solid;")
txtstream.WriteLine("    PADDING-RIGHT: 6px;")
txtstream.WriteLine("    PADDING-LEFT: 6px;")
txtstream.WriteLine("    FONT-WEIGHT: Normal;")
txtstream.WriteLine("    PADDING-BOTTOM: 6px;")
txtstream.WriteLine("    COLOR: white;")
txtstream.WriteLine("    PADDING-TOP: 6px;")
txtstream.WriteLine("    BORDER-BOTTOM: #999 1px solid;")
txtstream.WriteLine("    BACKGROUND-COLOR: navy;")
txtstream.WriteLine("    FONT-FAMILY: font-family: Cambria, serif;")
txtstream.WriteLine("    FONT-SIZE: 10px;")
txtstream.WriteLine("    text-align: left;")
txtstream.WriteLine("    white-Space: nowrap;")
```

```
txtstream.WriteLine("}")
txtstream.WriteLine("span")
txtstream.WriteLine("{")
txtstream.WriteLine("   BORDER-RIGHT: #999999 3px solid;")
txtstream.WriteLine("   PADDING-RIGHT: 3px;")
txtstream.WriteLine("   PADDING-LEFT: 3px;")
txtstream.WriteLine("   FONT-WEIGHT: Normal;")
txtstream.WriteLine("   PADDING-BOTTOM: 3px;")
txtstream.WriteLine("   COLOR: white;")
txtstream.WriteLine("   PADDING-TOP: 3px;")
txtstream.WriteLine("   BORDER-BOTTOM: #999 1px solid;")
txtstream.WriteLine("   BACKGROUND-COLOR: navy;")
txtstream.WriteLine("   FONT-FAMILY: font-family: Cambria, serif;")
txtstream.WriteLine("   FONT-SIZE: 10px;")
txtstream.WriteLine("   text-align: left;")
txtstream.WriteLine("   white-Space: nowrap;")
txtstream.WriteLine("   display: inline-block;")
txtstream.WriteLine("   width: 100%;")
txtstream.WriteLine("}")
txtstream.WriteLine("textarea")
txtstream.WriteLine("{")
txtstream.WriteLine("   BORDER-RIGHT: #999999 3px solid;")
txtstream.WriteLine("   PADDING-RIGHT: 3px;")
txtstream.WriteLine("   PADDING-LEFT: 3px;")
txtstream.WriteLine("   FONT-WEIGHT: Normal;")
txtstream.WriteLine("   PADDING-BOTTOM: 3px;")
txtstream.WriteLine("   COLOR: white;")
```

```
txtstream.WriteLine("    PADDING-TOP: 3px;")
txtstream.WriteLine("    BORDER-BOTTOM: #999 1px solid;")
txtstream.WriteLine("    BACKGROUND-COLOR: navy;")
txtstream.WriteLine("    FONT-FAMILY: font-family: Cambria, serif;")
txtstream.WriteLine("    FONT-SIZE: 10px;")
txtstream.WriteLine("    text-align: left;")
txtstream.WriteLine("    white-Space: nowrap;")
txtstream.WriteLine("    width: 100%;")
txtstream.WriteLine("}")
txtstream.WriteLine("select")
txtstream.WriteLine("{")
txtstream.WriteLine("    BORDER-RIGHT: #999999 3px solid;")
txtstream.WriteLine("    PADDING-RIGHT: 6px;")
txtstream.WriteLine("    PADDING-LEFT: 6px;")
txtstream.WriteLine("    FONT-WEIGHT: Normal;")
txtstream.WriteLine("    PADDING-BOTTOM: 6px;")
txtstream.WriteLine("    COLOR: white;")
txtstream.WriteLine("    PADDING-TOP: 6px;")
txtstream.WriteLine("    BORDER-BOTTOM: #999 1px solid;")
txtstream.WriteLine("    BACKGROUND-COLOR: navy;")
txtstream.WriteLine("    FONT-FAMILY: font-family: Cambria, serif;")
txtstream.WriteLine("    FONT-SIZE: 10px;")
txtstream.WriteLine("    text-align: left;")
txtstream.WriteLine("    white-Space: nowrap;")
txtstream.WriteLine("    width: 100%;")
txtstream.WriteLine("}")
txtstream.WriteLine("input")
```

```
txtstream.WriteLine("{")
txtstream.WriteLine("    BORDER-RIGHT: #999999 3px solid;")
txtstream.WriteLine("    PADDING-RIGHT: 3px;")
txtstream.WriteLine("    PADDING-LEFT: 3px;")
txtstream.WriteLine("    FONT-WEIGHT: Bold;")
txtstream.WriteLine("    PADDING-BOTTOM: 3px;")
txtstream.WriteLine("    COLOR: white;")
txtstream.WriteLine("    PADDING-TOP: 3px;")
txtstream.WriteLine("    BORDER-BOTTOM: #999 1px solid;")
txtstream.WriteLine("    BACKGROUND-COLOR: navy;")
txtstream.WriteLine("    FONT-FAMILY: font-family: Cambria, serif;")
txtstream.WriteLine("    FONT-SIZE: 12px;")
txtstream.WriteLine("    text-align: left;")
txtstream.WriteLine("    display: table-cell;")
txtstream.WriteLine("    white-Space: nowrap;")
txtstream.WriteLine("    width: 100%;")
txtstream.WriteLine("}")
txtstream.WriteLine("h1 {")
txtstream.WriteLine("color: antiquewhite;")
txtstream.WriteLine("text-shadow: 1px 1px black;")
txtstream.WriteLine("padding: 3px;")
txtstream.WriteLine("text-align: center;")
txtstream.WriteLine("box-shadow: inset 2px 5px rgba(0,0,0,0.5), inset -2px -2px 5px rgba(255,255,255,0.5);")
txtstream.WriteLine("}")
txtstream.WriteLine("</style>")
```